THE LAW FIRM GROWTH FORMULA

How smart solicitors attract more of the right clients
at the right price to grow their law firm quickly

NICK JERVIS
SOLICITOR (NON-PRACTISING)

R3THINK PRESS

First published in Great Britain 2017 by Rethink Press (www.rethinkpress.com)

For
Emma, Megan and Samuel: my world.

Praise

'As an owner or manager of your firm you want to achieve growth and then be able to "rinse and repeat". This book tells you how in a practical and methodical way and gives you the tools to own this process for yourself, whether you do it all for yourself or manage others to do some or all of it for you. It also gives you the tools to measure and manage your progress. A refreshing and useful business read and having tested the method I know it works."

MARIE HUNTLEY
Huntley Legal Solicitors

"A well-structured and easy to follow guide to growing your law firm. Nick avoids 'marketing speak' and instead uses straightforward and accessible language, making his ideas easy to follow and implement. Helpful, informative and a must read for any lawyer involved in business development."

JONATHAN TYLER
Partner, Seth Lovis & Co. Solicitors

"High Street law firms continue to be under increasing pressure. That is not going to change. Advice from Nick Jervis over the last eight years has been a critical factor in the growth of my successful and profitable practice, and his book is packed with practical marketing advice. If you want your law firm to prosper and thrive, you need to read this book."

TIM BISHOP
Senior Partner, Bonallack and Bishop

"It is clear that Nick really understands the legal services market and what it takes to make the telephone ring for solicitors. I have no doubt that any solicitor who wants to grow their law firm reads this and then takes action will see very impressive results. It is working for me!"

JONATHAN GOODWIN
Solicitor Advocate

"Nick Jervis has written a very comprehensive marketing guide which will surely be of immense value to anyone wishing to grow their practice. Nick has clearly drawn upon all his years of marketing experience to produce this practical and insightful guide, which is packed full of information including a selection of very handy marketing checklists designed to give structure, momentum and success.

Buy it!"

CHRIS CARTER
Carter & Carter Solicitors

"At last, a marketing book for lawyers written in plain English. Nick certainly gets to the point without resorting to marketing speak. You can look forward to learning about lots of simple, effective ideas to promote and grow your law firm. Packed with practical examples, this book provides a step by step guide to increase your turnover, profit and to enhance the reputation of your practice."

JACQUELINE EMMERSON
Director, Emmersons Solicitors

"What Nick Jervis has written here is a straightforward guide that will allow any law firm to put in place marketing that attracts new clients predictably and reliably. Everything in this book is rooted in experience not theory, and Nick does a great job of explaining everything clearly. Armed with this book alone, someone who's never marketed anything before would quickly be able to start generating good quality new leads and clients for their law firm."

MARK CREASER
Managing Partner, Ideal Result

Contents

Foreword

There are precious few books that focus on how to grow a law firm. Most sit in one of two camps: those that offer a snake-oil salesman's magic silver bullet ('double your profits in one month or your money back...') and those that are not rooted in the reality of what it is like to try and grow a law firm. I am delighted to say that *The Law Firm Growth Formula* is neither of these.

Nick Jervis has taken a practical and proven formula and explained how it can be applied to your law firm. He explains the steps and the processes and even explains how and why you should be using his tools.

This book is not about your technical ability to deliver your service; that is not in dispute. It is about your ability to run a business. It about getting you to work *On* your business and not just *In* the business. Easy to say and difficult to do.

Let's be clear, marketing is an entire waste of time if it doesn't result in a sale, now or in the future. Too much time is spent looking at vanity measures (hits, likes, follows) and not enough time is spent looking at how to increase sales to the clients you want to be working with. I am delighted to say that Nick is far more interested in what actually works to help you grow your practice.

In a light, yet engaging style, Nick manages to get to the essence of some core questions that can keep you awake at night:

- Why should people bother to buy from you when they can buy from the competition?
- What makes you different from the rest?
- How can you get more and better clients?
- How can you get more enquiries and how can you convert more of the ones you want?
- Which marketing tools should you use and how do you use them?

Answering these questions is especially difficult for a professional service firm. You are not selling a product that can be seen and touched; you are selling a service which feels near impossible to differentiate, one from another. I would go as far as to say that you are selling hot air: an idea, a belief that you are the best solution for a client. Being able to articulate what you do and why you should be selected is as important, if not more important than being able to do the work itself.

Nick's approach will underpin your ability to grow a more successful law firm. It will help you to run the firm you are capable of running. Along the way he will also challenge the role of your law firm and how you need to flex and adjust so that you don't get left behind in a world of incredibly high-paced change.

Every law firm should put up a copy of Nick's Client Conversion Flowchart in their office and issue everyone with a copy of his New Client Flowcast Marketing Model. If only more practices bought into such an approach then the industry would have a far better reputation for delivering responsive customer service and value for money!

Meanwhile, only those that know about Nick's charts will gain the benefits. And that is only as long as you actually take what he recommends and take the relevant action.

Every industry is vulnerable to being 'uberised'. Client needs and demands are rapidly changing as are their options for solutions.

In fact, there will inevitably be even more seismic changes in the industry. Not all firms will survive. Nick's book will help you to run a firm fit for the increasingly demanding world we now live and compete in.

I am more and more convinced that effective marketing is all about the execution of the plan. This book will show you what to do and how to do it!

Hope is not a strategy!

Robert Craven
Author, *Grow Your Service Firm*

Introduction

Who is this book for?

This book, and the formula contained within it, will work for anyone involved in the marketing of legal services. The marketing strategies and tactics I talk about have been used for law firms of all sizes, from sole practitioners to mid-tier and top tier law firms.

However, some of the specific elements of the book are aimed very much at the law firm owner. A law firm owner might work alone, or might employ a team of 20 to 100 staff in one or more offices, but the owner is the sole decision maker. Why do I specifically focus on this law firm owner? Well, you probably need to know a little bit about me to understand this better, so let me tell you a little about my background – and also about my impatience. That part is quite critical.

My Story

I entered the legal profession later in life than most. My impatience caused me to abandon my 'A' levels after only one year. I was frustrated at hearing more and more theory and not doing anything with it. I wanted to get out into the world and do something. I'd had jobs from about the age of 12 and I knew that I was a good worker, because I was constantly being told that this was the case wherever I worked, from the lovely lady at the end of my paper round who rewarded me with a milky coffee and occasionally a cake if I delivered the papers to her hotel before 7 AM, to the hotel owner in Devon where I worked part-time but ended up being the bar and restaurant manager because I worked so hard and well, via many other jobs in between. I knew I could turn my hand to most things and I seemed to do them well, so I was keen to do something full time and earn a living.

So, I walked away from my 'A' levels, much to the disappointment of my parents, and went to work in a transport company, renting out articulated trucks and trailers. I worked my way up to the position of Southern Area Relief Manager, but really couldn't see myself doing that for the rest of my life, so I left to travel and see some of the world.

After spending some time in Greece sailing yachts, I returned to the UK in my early 20s and decided it was about time I chose a career. However, as I was impatient there was no way that that career was going to involve returning to education in any way, shape or form, and studying full time. I needed to be working at the same time as learning a profession. I settled on the idea of becoming a legal executive and then going on to qualify as a solicitor. Once I had reached this decision, I just needed to find somewhere to work.

As I didn't have the patience to wait around for a recruitment company to find me a job, I hand-wrote 64 letters (I remember each and every one) to solicitors across the south and south west, and was finally offered an interview and then a job at a firm in Reading.

I began my remote Institute of Legal Executives studies as soon as possible, but at the same time I was keen to make myself useful at the firm where I was working. I set up a debt recovery department and quickly 'learned by doing' debt recovery and litigation.

Once I had started working in litigation, I decided that I would specialise in personal injury claims, which at the time seemed to be a growing area of legal services (it was, but is not so much anymore). However, the firm where I worked didn't really have enough work to allow me to do this. I could wait around and hope that that would change, but I think you know by now that wasn't going to happen. When I was offered a job elsewhere, at a firm that agreed to keep funding my studies, my current firm surprised me by saying they would rather keep me, let me generate my own caseload – and provide me with a marketing budget.

Another of the roles I had undertaken before joining the law had been working in marketing for the former owner of a London advertising agency. I had enjoyed it immensely, so this was just too good an offer for me to turn down. It wasn't that I didn't like working where I was, it was simply that they hadn't had the work that I wanted to do. Now that I was told I could create my own caseload and do my own marketing, I was a very happy man – well, most of the time anyway.

Which parts made me unhappy? Well, as I had a knack for marketing, I was soon undertaking marketing for the eight-partner firm across four locations. The parts that I found incredibly frustrating were the partner and committee meetings, where, in my humble opinion, nothing was ever achieved, or if it was it took about 300 hours longer than it should have done to reach a decision. I used to get so frustrated with the slow decision-making process that during one of these long-drawn-out meetings I actually prepared a dossier on how to run any meeting in less than 30 minutes and ensure you came out with decisions. I found it some years later and it did make me laugh.

My impatience was at the fore again when I started my law firm marketing consultancy in 2003, and I was quickly reminded of the frustrations of my practising days whenever I started working with any firm that had more than one partner.* Suddenly, what I had

---

* If you are operating in a partnership where every marketing decision needs the approval of all partners, you absolutely have to fix this. My solution is simple. One partner, that is probably you as you are reading this book, is given responsibility for all marketing for one year. He or she is given a budget, and carte blanche to make decisions and take action. At the end of that year the other partners look through the results. If the marketing has put more money into the bank than it took out (by a ratio of at least three to one) then let them carry on. Problem solved!

advised my clients was the best course of action would lead to a two-, three- or six-month debate, back and forth from meeting to meeting, about whether they should do what I was suggesting. It wasn't that they weren't paying me during this period – that wasn't the point. My joy from doing what I do comes from agreeing a course of action, implementing it, and then seeing the results and my clients' happiness with these results.

Getting Results

This is what drives me and keeps me going. The idea of taking six months to make a simple decision came close to driving me insane. As Einstein so eloquently said, doing the same thing over and over again and expecting different outcomes is the definition of insanity, so I knew that this could not continue.

I therefore made the decision to work in a consultancy capacity only with decision makers: people I could agree a course of action with knowing that they would instantly say yes, and that if they did so they wouldn't come back to me a few weeks later to say that their other partners had pooh-poohed our agreed plan of action. These people are as keen as I am to see results, and as they are not shackled by other partners they are able to take fast action, often leaving their competitors scratching their heads about how this once-small law firm now seems to be bigger than they are, yet still has only one equity partner.

It is not that I don't work in some capacity with larger firms; I do. I run AdWords campaigns for some of them, but only if the person I am working with has the power to make decisions on behalf of their department. I also have many larger firms that are members of my Marketing4Solicitors service, using my ideas to grow their law firm.

But in a consultancy capacity I will only work with someone who has the authority to make decisions and see them through to the end. My book is therefore geared towards them, because I know from many years' experience that I can transform their firm for them, and make their life a lot more enjoyable.

Let's look at how, shall we?

Chapter 1

The Law Firm
Growth Formula

This book contains a formula to grow your law firm. It is tried and tested. It works. Or to put it correctly: it works if you work it.

If you are absolutely committed to growing your law firm and are prepared to put in some time learning and applying this formula, you will be successful. I have used this system with my consultancy clients time and time again.

The *Only* time that it doesn't work is when a solicitor doesn't apply the formula consistently or follow the processes that they have put in place to make it work in the first place.

It is not that this formula is particularly convoluted or difficult, and the processes that you have to put in place are all relatively straightforward, but you do have to follow them and monitor the results consistently to ensure that you are continually growing your law firm. This is where many of the problems arise. A solicitor might start to follow the formula but then other 'stuff' gets in the way, or they decide to start a completely different marketing tactic that simply won't work, but because it looks more fun, they stop before they achieve the results that would otherwise follow. If I had a penny for every time a solicitor has said to me, 'But I really want to do some social media marketing because it looks so much fun, Nick', I would be very wealthy.

If I do not manage to convince them that social media alone will never transform a law firm, they go off and waste countless hours and often thousands of pounds on social media training and even a company to help them, before finally realising that it simply doesn't work (see Chapter 13 for the reasons why). However, following my formula does work.

You will no doubt have heard of the proverb that says if you give a man a fish you feed him for a day, but teach him to fish and you feed him for a lifetime.

With this book, I aim to go one step further for you and for your law firm. I want to teach you how to fish and then, more importantly, teach you how to employ fishermen to fish for you while you simply monitor them and watch your catch grow continually.

My aim for you is that you should do as little as possible when it comes to growing your law firm. I want you to be in control of everything that is happening, but actually doing very little to make it happen. It is when I achieve this with my law firm clients that they really start to enjoy running their law firm and living their life. My heartfelt desire is that you achieve both of these outcomes. If you are prepared to put in some time understanding the marketing tactics that really do work for law firms, then some more time implementing them for your firm (usually by outsourcing the whole or most of the day-to-day work), and then consistently tracking the results so that you can improve on them, you will succeed. You cannot fail to.

The reason that this formula is so important is because it will replace the usual method by which law firms to attempt to grow, which I have seen so many times and which leads only to frustration, limited results and often also to burnout.

The Law Firm Marketing Roller Coaster

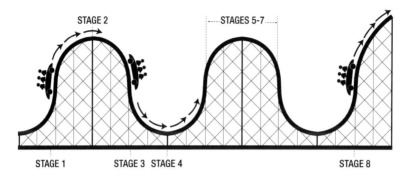

Let's look at each stage of the The Law Firm Marketing Roller Coaster in turn.

STAGE 1: You have no clients. You start frantically looking for clients. You contact old clients, referrers and start advertising anywhere that you can think of to make your telephone ring. You work tirelessly to achieve some new client instructions.

STAGE 2: Eventually your endeavours pay off (although you are not sure what worked exactly). You have more work than you can handle, for now at least. You ease back on the marketing so that you can concentrate on the work.

STAGE 3: Your instructions start to dwindle; you are coming down the other side of the marketing roller coaster hill and it doesn't feel good. You are sure it will pick up soon though, but it doesn't, so you career towards stage 4.

STAGE 4: You are back where you started, so you do what you did at the beginning and start marketing frantically.

STAGE 5–7: Exactly the same thing happens again over the next few months. You become too busy again because of your frantic marketing activity, so you stop marketing and start heading downwards on the marketing roller coaster. When you reach the bottom, you start marketing again, then stop again when you reach the bottom of the roller coaster. You are tired, bored and frustrated at your lack of progress. You decide that there has to be a better way. There is: the law firm growth formula, and you commit to applying it to your law firm.

STAGE 8: With a strong commitment to break your current cycle of feast and famine, you implement the law firm growth formula one step at a time until you start to see a consistent rise to success. Your volume of instructions simply keeps increasing. You are not coming down the other side of this marketing roller coaster any longer because you are now following a proven formula.

Let's take a look at the formula.

The Law Firm Growth Formula

The law firm growth formula entails:

1. measuring your current performance accurately, so that you can then improve your results;
2. implementing improvements to your current 'client conversion process', that is, the system that you follow to convert a prospect into a client (whether you have committed this system to paper or not);
3. adding new marketing arteries from the New Client Flowcast, a.k.a. 'with or without you' (WOWY) marketing (post);
4. continually monitoring your performance;
5. adding new marketing arteries, or, when they are all in place, ensuring that you are optimising them before moving onto the marketing capillaries to help you reach your new, now expanded, goals; and
6. changing your goals as your law firm grows.

I have used some terminology here that might need some further explanation, so read on.

The Client Conversion Process

The 'client conversion process' is the system that you follow to move the client along the path from being someone in need of legal services to the point where they instruct your firm to represent them. In my experience, very few firms actually have any system for recording this process, and worse still, those that do rarely manage to follow it, which is a huge and costly mistake.

Implementing a 'client conversion process 'and then following it, alongside constantly trying to make small improvements, is certain to lead to increased income from people who have already found your law firm.

Increasing income through improving conversion rates

Service Provided	Number of Enquiries Per Month	Average Costs Per Client	Current Percentage Conversion rate (ie enquiries/ clients x 100)	Costs Per Month	Conversion rate after implement changes	Increase in Costs Per Month	Increase in Costs Per Month
Con-veyanc-ing	20	£500	30% (6 clients)	£3,000	50% (10 clients)	£2,000	£24,000
Employ-ment Law	20	£750	30% (6 clients)	£4,500	50% (10 clients)	£3,000	£36,000
Per-sonal Injury	20	£1,500	30% (6 clients)	£9,000	50% (10 clients)	£6,000	£72,000
Probate	20	£3,000	30% (6 clients)	£18,000	50% (10 clients)	£12,000	£144,000
Wills	20	£150	30% (6 clients)	£900	50% (10 clients)	£600	£7,200

Looking at the table above, you can see what a difference it can make to your financial health if you can make even small improvements to your conversion percentage, which is calculated in the following way:

Number of people instructing you **divided by** number of people enquiring about your services **multiplied by** 100

Therefore, if 50 people enquire about your services in any given month, but only 10 people instruct you, your conversion rate will be 10/50 × 100 = 20%.

I will show you in more detail how to measure this and then, far more importantly, how to improve on it, so that you can generate more income from the people who already find your law firm but are choosing not to instruct you. This is the fastest way to increase your income. It costs you very little aside from your time to implement the improvements, so it is an incredibly important part of my formula.

If you miss this part out, you will be throwing away instructions month by month. This is bad enough if you do not have many of the marketing arteries from the New Client Flowcast model (below) in place, but if you then add more of the arteries to your system without improving your client conversion process, you will waste more money every month as you fail to convert even more potential clients into new instructions.

The New Client Flowcast

Before I explain the New Client Flowcast and show you a diagram, let me explain something that might surprise, and even please, you. Most law firms can thrive by implementing just three or four marketing tactics. Whether you are a sole practitioner or a thriving mid-level law firm, there will usually only be three or four marketing tactics that regularly produce new client instructions of any magnitude.

Does that surprise you? I can tell you that it surprised me when I really started studying marketing many years ago. At the law firm I first worked for, all of our clients came in via three or four regular marketing tactics.

When I established my consultancy in 2003, I thought I might find that other firms needed many more, but that isn't the case at all. When applied well, three or four marketing tactics are usually all that is needed.

I will explain in detail which three or four later in the book, but for now I simply want to explain the New Client Flowcast and how it works.

The New Client Flowcast

In the diagram above, look at the main river: it represents your profits, and it is filled by your flow of new client instructions. What makes these clients come to you? Your marketing arteries and capillaries.

There are four marketing arteries. These are the four most effective marketing methods for solicitors in my automated marketing strategy for growth; here they are:

- A website that is designed to make your telephone ring and grows consistently;
- An email marketing database and monthly email;
- Google AdWords; and
- Referrals.

I also call my automated marketing strategy With Or Without You (wowy) marketing, because just like one of the great Irish rock bands more famous songs, it keeps on bringing new clients to your door every month *With Or Without You.* WOWY marketing is crucial to the savvy law firm business owner, because it allows them to scale up their law firm without making themselves a slave to it.

My mission in life is to enable solicitors to have a thriving law firm at the same time as being able to live a good and a full life. So often over the years I have met law firm owners who come to me at the point of 'burn out', caused by trying to grow their law firm or even by just trying to keep it going. That is no absolutely no way to live. In my opinion, we get just one shot at this planet earth thing, so why make it a long, hard slog when it can be a blissful jog?

It doesn't have to be like this. You can grow your firm and live a good and happy life if you spend some time implementing the right WOWY marketing for your law firm.

I will show you how to do this in the later chapters, but I wanted you to know right now that there is a better and easier way for you to grow your firm than you might have been experiencing up until this point.

What Gets Measured Gets Better

If you want to know which of your marketing methods are working and which are costing you money with absolutely no results, you must live by my saying that 'What gets measured gets better'. Measure every marketing activity you undertake. If it is not bringing in more fees than it costs, change and improve it. If you still can't make it work after changing and improving it several times, stop it and try something else.

This is such a simple point yet it is in nearly every case overlooked by law firms, either deliberately because it seems too much like 'hard work' or, usually, through blind ignorance. Sorry to be brutal, but my job here is to point out where you have been going wrong and to ensure you change your ways to build the practice of your dreams.

The great news is that it really isn't hard to measure where all your new business is coming from, so the small amount of hard work to start doing this now will reward you many times over in the future with new clients and will also save you from wasting your hard-earned money on marketing that simply isn't working.

Chapter 2

Your Growth Mantra

Now this is not a heavy, dull, traditional marketing book with lots of complicated definitions and systems that will mean nothing to you. All these types of textbooks are dry, dull and mostly irrelevant to what you need to know to run a successful business. They might help you to pass an exam, just like the law books I was forced to study for years to qualify as a solicitor, but once you have passed your exams you can forget about using the textbooks to help you in your day-to-day job because they mean nothing in the real world!

There are so many different definitions for marketing, and some of them are long and convoluted enough to curdle milk. I believe that my job is to make it easy for my clients to 'get it'. Here is the only definition and checklist, rolled into one, that you will ever need for marketing your law firm:

Clients First!

If you put your clients first in all that you do and say, you will have great success when it comes to marketing your business. Every single time you provide your legal services, write a page for your website, prepare an advertisement, write a direct mail letter or an email newsletter for your clients, you must read it back and say, 'Have I put my Clients First?' If not, you need to go back and rewrite it.

In the world in which we now live, where reviews posted online remain there forever more, it is absolutely critical that the legal services you provide are as good as they can be.

Whenever you are providing your service, ask yourself this question and genuinely mean it: 'How can I make this service better and easier for my clients?' This question alone, if used regularly, can and will add more clients into your law firm.

In the marketing context, let me give you an example of how this might work in practice. On a law firm website, the opening paragraph on the home page might well be as follows:

'We were established in 1840 in our offices in Basingstoke...'

On reading that, ask yourself if the clients are being put first in that opening line? No – the opening is all about the law firm and nothing to do with their clients, isn't it? If I am a potential client of that firm, why does it matter that they have been there since 1840? It doesn't really, in the way it is presented above, but it could be given meaning for me as a potential client if it were changed as follows:

> **'If you are a small business we can save you thousands of pounds of unnecessary tax and expenses every single year, using our expertise gained from helping businesses for over 100 years.'**

Now that puts clients first, doesn't it? If you are a small business, you are now thinking 'tell me more', aren't you?

With reference to my own business I could say:

> **'I established my law firm marketing consultancy in 2003 to use all of my legal marketing expertise to help solicitors to grow their practices.'**

That's a bit 'me, me, me' though isn't it? It would be better if I said this, would it not?

> **'If you own or run a law firm and are looking to grow it substantially, I can show you exactly what you need to do to achieve this.'**

Put your clients first, always, and everything in your practice from this moment onwards will be a lot easier for you.

Chapter 3

Why Should I Choose Your Law Firm?

This is a really important question for you to ask yourself. It is not one for you to brush off, thinking that it doesn't apply to you. If you can't answer this question, why should you expect your clients to choose you? Quite simply, they won't. You must be able to answer this question.

For my business, I think I have nailed this now.

Q Why should someone choose me?

A You should work with me if you are the owner or major decision maker of a law firm and you are serious about growing your law firm quickly.

So how can you explain in a few words exactly why a client should choose you? The good news – it is really quite simple, so let me show you exactly how you do this.

You may see the title of this chapter and think that it is not a very glamorous or exciting chapter, or that it will not teach you anything new, or immediately help you to sell more of your services, but I can absolutely guarantee you that it will.

Unless and until you understand how to write or talk about your services in the right frame for your clients, selling your services across every type of media will always be far more difficult than it need be. You will end up spending more money on printed media, more money online, and more money on every type of marketing tactic that you undertake just to keep your telephone ringing.

However, when you understand how important your message is, everything else you do will become so much more effective. You will be able to spend less on marketing to acquire more clients.

So what do I mean when I use the 'sales' word that solicitors generally do not like to use, and tell you that you need to 'Craft' a compelling sales message to attract and convert more clients'? Surely you supply legal services and the world should be buying them from you and only you? Wouldn't that be nice?

Unfortunately, the world has changed, and whereas the sign 'Solicitors' above an office door used to be enough to have people finding you day in and day out, clients have become a lot more discerning, a lot harder to attract and then convert into new instructions, and less loyal than they ever used to be, even when you do win their business.

If you think about the sector that has perhaps had the most media coverage (not necessarily in a good way) and faced the biggest changes, the personal injury sector, there is an interesting lesson to learn. The personal injury sector has seen major upheaval, and claims companies were at the heart of this. Why, you might ask yourself – as I know a lot of solicitors did – were claims companies able to come into an established market and attract clients away from solicitors, then sell their instruction back to solicitors?

I think the major point is that they got their message right. They understood how to attract and convert clients better than solicitors. If this were not true, clients would have continued to go straight to the solicitors.

There were other factors, too, that created this new tier, or obstruction, in the personal injury sector:

- Claims companies set aside large marketing budgets to attract new clients, and solicitors were not doing this.
- Claims companies understood that one of the ongoing fears that prevented clients from contacting a solicitor was that it would cost them money.
- Claims companies made their sales message very easy to understand. They highlighted that all initial enquiries were free and claims were made on a 'no win, no fee' basis.

Of course, we all know that in many cases there was a lot of small print, leading to the client losing a lot of compensation, but this just highlights the point of how important it is to get your 'opening message' right. If you do not get this right, you miss the chance to win the client's instructions for good.

You can say the same about the Wills market, with unregulated Will writers, and even now about the business-to-business legal services market, with the selling of employment law services by the likes of Peninsula and many others.

These companies have come into the established legal services market, crafted a compelling message, and taken business away from solicitors. They have often packaged the service differently, or priced it differently, as with Peninsula, but ultimately it is the same service but sold with a different sales message.

If you can get your sales message right, you will maintain and strengthen your position, so that you can attract as many clients as you want and need to run a successful and profitable practice.

What Is Your Compelling Sales Message?

So, what am I looking to help you to achieve now? At the end of this section I expect you to be able to summarise in one sentence why I should choose your firm over and above your competitors in a way that appeals to your ideal clients.

You must be able to convey concisely and clearly who you work with and how you help them, so that if I stumble across your website, see your advertisement in the local paper, or meet you in person at a networking or social event, you can summarise why you are the best, and the only, firm to help me with my current legal needs.

Once you have this initial summary, you will need to develop your message beyond a single sentence so that it runs through all of your marketing materials, from your website to your brochures, and from your advertisements to your office window displays.

Let me show you some real examples of what you can create after you have completed this exercise, to help you to see why it can be so powerful.

Employment law solicitor: 'We only act for employees!'
This removes all ambiguity, making the marketing message so much clearer and resulting in more instructions.

Conveyancing solicitor: 'We will never pay estate agents for referrals, which means our advice is totally tailored to your needs.'
This removes any undue pressure from a third party that may conflict with your clients' interests. Surely that makes complete sense? Yet so many solicitors do pay referral fees to an agent, who so often has interests contradictory to those of their client.

Personal injury solicitor: 'You will always keep 100% of your compensation.'
If this had been on solicitors' lists of top five benefits they would never have accepted work from Claims Direct or The Accident Group. However, as we know, many solicitors did and this cost them dearly in the long run in so many ways.

Having this compelling sales message would also have allowed solicitors to promote this message heavily, at the expense of claims companies that did not operate in this way.

Overall, understanding what makes you different or attractive to your clients can have a dramatic impact on all of your marketing activities in many obvious ways (and many subtle ones, too, as shown above).

How to Craft Your Compelling Message

The next stage is to identify how and why you are different from your competitors so that you can create your compelling sales message.

I will provide you with the tools to do this easily, so do not worry if this sounds like hard work; it will not be. I know that you are good at the service you provide, but that you have probably been too modest and perhaps unable to summarise succinctly why you are the best firm for your clients. This will not be the case after working through the next stage.

Whenever you are thinking about marketing your legal practice, always, always, always think 'Clients First' before finalising your marketing activity. Does what you are saying or have written speak solely and squarely in terms of the benefits that your clients will receive if they use your service over and above the service offered by your competitors? If not, go back to the drawing board and start again until you can read back your message and nod your head because it speaks soundly and squarely to your ideal client.

There are two simple steps to creating your sales message/'why choose us' statement.

First, you use your own understanding of why you believe that you are good at the service that you provide. Second, you use your clients' feedback to ensure that you are on the right track. Don't worry, I am not talking about running a live client workshop here, just asking you to draw on feedback that you already have received from your clients for a job well done.

Identifying the areas in which you excel is crucial and will be very informative for you. I have performed this exercise with hundreds of solicitors. Some find it easy, others really struggle. All that I know is that every time it is performed, it is a real eye opener for the participants. I know that it will be the same for you too.

I am a bit of a traditionalist in many ways, despite my love of technology, so my advice is to print off the following table and head off to a quiet space such as your library or your favourite coffee shop to work through the exercise. Don't do it at your desk – the marketing mindset is very different from the one you use to work on legal matters.

Compelling Sales Message Exercise

The first exercise is to grab a sheet of A4 and draw three columns in it so that it looks like the table below (alternatively, head to the book resources section at www.samsonconsulting.co.uk/growth and you will find a prepared 'Features to Benefits' Word document that you can download and print off.)

Features to benefits

Features	Features to benefits conversion statement	Benefits
We were formed in 1832	this means that	We have substantial experience that we can use to ensure your transaction proceeds as smoothly and efficiently as possible.

Step 1: What are you good at?

Write everything down that comes to mind in terms of what makes your law firm special in the 'features' column'. Do not stop writing until you have put down at least 20 reasons, but possibly as many as 50. Give yourself at least 30 minutes to do this. It will be time well spent.

Ideally you should run out of ideas before seeking help from my list of questions below, to ensure that you haven't missed anything, so I have put my prompt sheet over the page in the hope that you will draw on your own ideas first.

When you have exhausted your own list (and only then), use my list of questions to help you to come up with more. (You can download a version to print here: www.samsonconsulting .co.uk/growth).

Did you look ahead? Oh dear – it is only yourself you are fooling if you did, but here is some help for you if you haven't yet come up with 50 reasons why a client should choose your law firm.

Features Checklist

- How long have you been in business?
- How big are you?
- How small are you?
- Do you serve any niche business areas?
- What are your opening hours?
- Do you have a Freephone telephone number?
- What are your client service level standards?
  - Calls answered within X rings
  - Letters replied to within Y days
  - Emails replied to within Z minutes
- Why should you be the business of choice for your clients?
- Who are your best known clients?
- If you have a questionnaire for clients, how often do you receive 10 out of 10 or excellent?
- What geographical areas do you cover?
- What legal services do you provide?
- Do you work well with any special categories of clients or niche businesses?
- Do you work well with any special categories of referrers?
- Are you the cheapest?
- Are you the most expensive?
- Are you the fastest?
- Are you the most thorough?
- Are you the friendliest?

Step 2: Features to benefits conversion table

Now that you have your lovely long list of features, you need to turn these into the corresponding benefit to your client. Most solicitors think of features, whereas all your clients want to know is what the 'benefit' for them is, or in other words, what's in it for them?

For example, you may have said that your firm was formed in 1832, which probably matters a great deal to you, but is largely irrelevant to your clients. For them, the year of your firm coming into being is not important; all that they care about is why you are the best solicitor for their job in hand. So how do you turn 1832 from a feature into a benefit? You use the feature-to-benefit conversion statement 'this means that', contained in the 'Features to benefits' table above, to arrive at the following:

> **We were formed in 1832. This means that we have substantial experience, which we use to ensure your transaction proceeds as smoothly and efficiently as possible.**

Suddenly, what was just a feature now speaks to your client in terms of why they should choose your firm.

This exercise helps you to understand why, in your clients' eyes you are the right solicitor for them. Once you have completed this exercise for all of your features, you will have gained a much deeper understanding of your firm. You now have to do some culling of your list to narrow it down to a smaller list, but one that contains all of your most powerful benefits.

First, quickly strike through any benefit that you realise is not of great value to your clients until you have around ten or twelve strong benefits.

Step 3: Using your clients to confirm your choices
Now it is time to run your answers past those of your clients. How?

Think of three matters that you have completed in the last few months that have had a great reaction or response from the client. If you do not earn fees any more, ask your fee earners to provide this information.

If the client provided a written letter of thanks, excellent. However, more often than not it will be face-to-face or telephone feedback, so get your team to summarise this feedback in writing so that you can compare it against your own results in the exercise above.

This is a crucial part of the exercise, so please do not skip it. I mentioned at the beginning that this really will dramatically improve the results of all of your marketing activities from this moment onwards, so a little time spent now will pay you back many, many times over.

Choose your top five benefits

Once you have completed this exercise, it is time to pick the top five reasons why clients choose your law firm. Go through the responses received from your clients and compare them with your own list of 10 or 12 benefits to see which ones match most closely the ones that your clients highlighted in their feedback of your services.

Remember that your clients are the most important people in this equation, so if you see a common response from your clients on a particular aspect of your service that could be a real hidden gem, you need to incorporate this into your list.

You can learn so much from your existing clients that will help you to secure many new clients like them in the future, so please make sure you always listen to them.

Ideal Client Feedback

The final stage involves obtaining some one-to-one client feedback to make sure you are selecting the benefits that will appeal most to your future clients.

You should have some clients that are your ideal clients. They provide you with regular instructions and refer you to other people or businesses. You like working with them and you wish you had more clients just like them. You need to ask them to look at your list of five benefits and ask them which of the benefits are the most important items on the list for them, and whether there are any others that they would add.

You only need to do this with three or four clients to confirm that you have chosen the right benefits.

NOTE: If during these discussions with your clients they offer you some feedback along the lines of 'I really liked the way you...' please immediately ask them to put that in writing to you. You can never have enough client reviews.

Your Final Statement

You will now have your final list of benefits, as approved by your ideal clients. Now is the time to print them out and keep them to hand so that you can quickly check back whenever you are preparing any marketing materials for your firm, to ensure that you are 'on message'.

For Larger Firms

If you are a large firm with many different departments providing different legal services I suggest that you follow this process:

1. Go through the steps above first when referring to the firm as a whole, so you have an understanding of your core sales message across the board.
2. Repeat the process for each of your areas of expertise so that you are then creating a compelling sales message for each of your legal services.

Implement

Now that you have clearly defined your service offering, what are you going to do with all of this information?

Over the course of the next few weeks you will need to make changes to all of your marketing materials. If you have done this exercise thoroughly, you will find that many of your marketing communications do not accurately reflect the major benefits of your services to your clients, so you need to correct this.

Review everything and ensure that your message is consistent in all of the following places:

- Your website
- Your new client letters
- Your advertising
- Your printed media (brochures, leaflets, etc.)
- Your message when you are out and about networking

Remember, if your message does not convey the benefits of your service to your clients, you are wasting your money!

Your Service Summary

Once you have finished the exercise above it is worth turning your key features and benefits into a useful sales aid that can be used whenever you are talking about your practice.

You may well have heard of the one-minute pitch, or 'elevator pitch', as it is known across the pond. The scenario is that you are given just one minute to pitch your business to potentially your biggest client: what are you going to say?

This may not be the way it was intended to be used, but I find that when I take solicitors through this exercise and they repeat the process several times, they feel much more comfortable answering the inevitable question 'So what is it that you do, then?'

I don't like to think of the outcome as a 'sales pitch', as I know many solicitors are horrified by that word, but as more of a 'service summary'. So how do you write your service summary?

Quite simply, I suggest that you answer these three questions:

1. Who do you serve?
2. What results do you achieve for them?
3. How can you prove this by referencing a recent client experience?

For my business, answering these three questions leads to this statement:

I work with law firm owners who want to grow their law firm. I tell them what to do, how to do it and how to outsource it all quickly so that it happens with or without them. One client recently trebled their turnover in a matter of months.

The equivalent statement for a law firm might be:

We work with small businesses who need prompt and practical legal solutions. We discover what is important to them so that we can provide them with the best legal solution while they concentrate on running their business. We recently avoided costly and lengthy litigation for one of our clients, saving them in excess of £10,000 and several months fighting a case with a supplier.

I can't overstate how useful it is to go through this exercise several times, to become really comfortable with the benefits you are offering to your clients.

Once you have done this, it is a good idea to write a different summary for each of your different areas of law, so that you have a good answer whenever you are asked what you do. The more you practice this the easier it becomes. In time, you will find that you can shorten this to the point of one sentence, or in my case four words: fast law firm growth!

My service offering has gone through many re-incarnations, and this one, for now, sums up what I do in all aspects of my business. You will be able to do the same for your practice and service summary too.

Chapter 4

How Many of Your Prospects Become Clients?

Whenever I visit a new legal practice I am often asked which is the first 'new' marketing activity that they should undertake to generate new clients for the firm? 'Shall we try social media marketing, or radio, Google AdWords or Facebook advertising?' The answer is always the same: 'None of the above.'

Improving New Client Conversion Processes

I know that I can help any law firm to generate more new client instructions more quickly simply by improving the process they follow for dealing with all new client enquiries. I also know that this is one of the most profitable uses of their time, as it costs the firm little or nothing to do, yet provides huge financial benefits in terms of new instructions received.

So, if this is the case, why do firms often show such reluctance to do this? I believe it is because this is not particularly exciting.

However, the longer I am involved in the marketing of legal services, the more I appreciate that it is the drilling down to these finer details that spells the difference between those firms doing incredibly well and those just getting by.

Which do you want to be?

I want to give you two explanations for how improving the way you deal with all new client enquiries can have such a dramatic impact on the success of your practice, making every marketing activity so much more effective for you. I appreciate that some people like figures, others like stories, so as I aim to please, here is an example in each category for you.

Number Crunching

Here is a simple table showing how getting this right can make a large and almost immediate impact to your monthly finances. I have included a range of different services, so you should be able to see how much of an impact you could have on your practice, depending on how many of the services you provide.

Projected income from increases in conversion rates

Service Provided	Number of Enquiries Per Month	Average Costs Per Client	Current Percentage Conversion rate (ie enquiries/ clients x 100)	Costs Per Month	Conversion Rate After Implement Changes	Increase in Costs Per Month	Increase in Costs Per Month
Conveyancing	20	£500	30% (6 clients)	£3,000	50% (10 clients)	£2,000	**£24,000**
Employment Law	20	£750	30% (6 clients)	£4,500	50% (10 clients)	£3,000	**£36,000**
Personal Injury	20	£1,500	30% (6 clients)	£9,000	50% (10 clients)	£6,000	**£72,000**
Probate	20	£3,000	30% (6 clients)	£18,000	50% (10 clients)	£12,000	**£144,000**
Wills	20	£150	30% (6 clients)	£900	50% (10 clients)	£600	**£7,200**

These are modest enquiry numbers, so are completely achievable. I appreciate that you might only offer one service, but even so there are considerable improvements to be made. If you offer several services, you can see that it can have a dramatic impact on your turnover and profitability.

In terms of conversion, improving your conversion rate from 30% to 50% is also achievable; I have done it now with enough firms to know this. These are realistic figures and they can be achieved by your firm if you set your mind to achieving them.

New Client Narrative

For those of you not quite so interested in the financial side of things, but much more so in the provision of a great service for your clients, here is a scenario based on my experience over the years both of engaging legal services for myself and also doing some mystery shopping for my clients. It is a very common scenario. My only question to you is, which firm are you?

Yvonne's choice

Yvonne is a married mother of three children; her family are in the process of moving house.

She asks her friends if they can recommend a solicitor but none has used one recently so cannot help.* Yvonne decides to call three local firms that she has found on the internet.

Smithers Jones is the first firm she calls. They have the most professional-looking website and she can tell they keep it up to date because they have a great blog and some really useful information to download about the house moving process. She expects that as

---

* Interestingly, in polls people say that they would go on a recommendation if they needed a solicitor, but when people who have actually instructed a solicitor are asked how they found them, recommendation is very low on the list. I am certain that the reason for this is that people do not use a solicitor regularly and therefore if someone asks for a recommendation they cannot help them because they do not remember the name of a law firm (unless of course the solicitor they used has read this book in which case they can easily recommend a firm because they send a very informative and useful monthly newsletter).

long as the price is not too much more than the other firms she is going to call she will use this firm.

She calls them and has a very satisfactory conversation with Mrs Jones. The price sounds reasonable and within 10 minutes of the end of the call she has an email quotation from them. She is suitably impressed.

Bradley Smythe is the next firm she calls. Their website is not as good as Smithers Jones's, but is updated regularly. However, it does not offer any extra useful information. The price is slightly cheaper than Smithers Jones, but Smithers Jones remain the favourites, particularly when Yvonne receives no email confirming the price or providing contact details following the call with Bradley Smythe.

Michael Smith is the last solicitor she calls. She thought of not bothering to call him as she is bored with speaking to solicitors now, but decided to force herself to do so [I know from my own experience that this is exactly how you begin to feel when choosing a solicitor]. She can tell from the website that he is a sole practitioner. His website is not quite so comprehensive as the others, in fact it is quite sparse, just listing the services provided, a few testimonials and contact details, but she likes the fact that it is easy to find a picture of the man she will be speaking to and that the firm prides itself on a very personal and professional service.

Michael Smith's price is the same as Smithers Jones's, but he seemed far more interested in finding out why Yvonne was moving and what deadlines were important to her. He spent longer on the telephone with her than the other two firms put together, but mostly he was talking about her needs, so the time went quickly. He confirmed a price and an email arrived within the hour. She was now torn between Smithers Jones and Michael Smith. She decided to make her final decision in a couple of days.

The next morning a letter arrived from Michael Smith, confirming the quotation that he had provided on the telephone. He also enclosed a brochure about his services that included a lot of feedback from satisfied clients. She was suitably impressed, particularly as she did not receive anything from the other two firms. She expected to receive their letters the next day. Michael Smith was clearly the favourite now.

> Two days passed and she had received nothing else from the other two firms. She was about to call Michael Smith to confirm she would like to him to help her to move house when her telephone rang: 'Hello Yvonne, this is Michael Smith. I am just calling to check you received my letter and quotation, and to see if you had any unanswered questions that I can help you with?'
>
> Michael Smith was duly instructed!

Which Firm Are You?

If the figures did not convince you that improving your process for dealing with new client enquiries is essential, I hope that this very real case study did.

I run a service for solicitors called Marketing4Solicitors. Through this service they receive access to online marketing precedents, training videos, and the ability to ask me questions. I ran a survey with my Marketing4Solicitors members and these were the results on follow up of new enquiries:

Always follow up	8%
Sometimes follow up	17%
Never follow up	75%

If you bear in mind that Marketing4Solicitors members are probably in the top 10% of forward-thinking law firms, this figure absolutely terrifies me. It is why this chapter is so important.

The changes this chapter recommends involve only a nominal investment, yet they make every other marketing activity that you undertake far more successful, that is, they provide you with more clients for no extra spend, so it is vital that you take action once you have read this chapter.

Choosing a solicitor is 'an informed decision': your prospects are making an informed decision about which solicitor they believe will do the best job possible for them. They can only base this decision on what you say and what you do. We all know that actions speak much louder than words.

Remember, I am buying/choosing a professional services provider. I expect you to show me how professional you are in all that you do, from start to finish, so surely an email, letter and follow-up telephone call is the minimum I should expect from you when I make an enquiry about your services, isn't it?

Start Measuring

Your First Measure

You have to begin by measuring your current position first so that you have a starting point. Then you simply work on improving that position.

You need, therefore, to start is by counting your current enquiries and calculating how many of those turn into new clients.

> **New client instructions ÷ by new enquiries received × 100
> = your current conversion rate**

Continue to do this for a couple of months to build up a picture of the average conversion rates you are achieving. This will provide you with your 'baseline', that is, the conversion rate you will now constantly try to beat by improving your processes.

If you are a sole practitioner, you will be able to introduce new client procedures very easily. If you are a larger firm with several departments, you might choose to start with one department, then roll out the process once you see how effective it is. If you decide to do it this way, I strongly advise you to start in the department with the highest average fee per transaction. This way you will see some very pleasing results in terms of increases in income!

Your next measure

Once you have your baseline, you can start to implement the changes suggested in this chapter, and once you have done this, continue to assess your conversion rate on a month by month basis.

Once you get past the initial inertia experienced when setting up any new process, this will become second nature. It is a process that every law firm should undertake, but I know most do not. It will put you at a distinct advantage over your competition and will be an invaluable use of your time.

Even when you can see the impact your changes are making, continue to tweak your new client conversion process – this should never stop. If you can keep making small adjustments that improve your conversion rates, your bottom line profits will continue to rise. Keep going, always.

One thing is certain: once you start to apply the changes in this chapter you will see an improvement in your conversion rate, which in turn means an improvement in your profits.

Chapter 5

Improving Your Client Conversion Process

... or: more client instructions at no extra cost from people already contacting you!

Now that you know how many of your prospects turn into new clients, it is vital that you put in place a process to improve your current numbers.

I understand that solicitors rarely like to think of themselves as sales people, but the world has changed, and you now have to be able to present your services and deliver them in a way that makes them attractive to clients, and, most importantly, makes them choose you over and above your competition.

Therefore, it is vital that you have a client conversion process to ensure that you turn more of the people asking about your services into new client instructions. You will in fact already have a client conversion process; it is just that you have probably never called it that before. So, what is it?

In short, it is your prospective client's journey from the first contact with you (which might be on your website, reading an advertisement, or even walking past your offices) until the moment that they either instruct you (if you do this well) or one of your competitors.

This section deals with each stage of the process, from the moment your potential client hears about your services right up until the final decision. When I say 'hears about your service', I mean the very first second that they hear about you, which is often long before they pick up the telephone to you or fill in an enquiry form on your website, because one of the most important parts of the process starts before they even see your promotional materials.

What Are You Selling?

What do you sell? What is the purpose of your website, your newspaper advertisements or a direct mail letter that you send out to your ideal prospects? If I ask this at a live event or in person, the first answer that comes back is that you are selling your legal services. This is wrong. Totally wrong.

You never sell your legal services from any of your marketing materials. Let me explain what I mean here, as I appreciate that this does seem to be counter-intuitive:

> **The only purpose of any of your marketing is
> to sell the first contact with your firm.**

That is all that you are trying to sell: first contact with you. If you were selling pet food, you would try to sell your products from an advertisement or from your website. You can also take this approach with books (Amazon seem to do quite well with these), or with cosmetics, toiletries or chocolates. When you are buying products, it is easy to manage the entire sales process without any human interaction.

However, when you are selling services, especially legal services, human interaction is the most important part of the process. There will be a tiny part of the population who would be happy to buy a legal service on price alone, without any human interaction, but I can promise you that it is just that: a tiny percentage.

Even if you sell more commoditised services such as Will writing or conveyancing, human contact is a vital part of the process if you want to charge a reasonable price for your services, which, as a professional service provider, you absolutely must do.

This is why clients who have followed my advice and implemented changes are able to charge more for Wills and conveyancing than their competitors, and still improve their conversion rates. It totally puts to bed the ridiculous notion that you can only sell conveyancing or Wills based on price, which I have heard far too many times from people who should know better. If you were in this camp before reading that last paragraph, I am delighted to advise you that you are wrong.

Follow the process outlined in the rest of this chapter and you will be very pleasantly surprised when, in a few weeks' time, you are quoting and converting at a much higher rate than you currently are doing. I have gone through this process with so many solicitors now that I promise you this is true. I have clients selling conveyancing services at fees 20–100% higher than they were doing previously because they have finally invested the time to put in place this simple process that allows them to charge a reasonable fee for their specialist services.

Back to the client conversion process: all your marketing should be solely focused on one of only two things:

- making your telephone ring; or
- encouraging your prospective client to make contact with you from your website (via an enquiry form, email or live chat).

When writing content for your advertisements or for your website, please remember this crucial point: you are writing the content with the sole intention of encouraging your prospect to get in touch with you. This means that you must do all of these things:

- convince your prospects that you understand their needs;
- convince your prospects that you are worthy of their business (i.e. that you are experts in this area of law);
- show them that you have done this before for other people just like them (reviews);
- explain that all initial contact is free of charge; and
- make it obvious how they can get in touch with you and provide them with a range of methods for doing so.

You don't need to go into the detail of how you will handle the service, or spell out the legal aspects of it; these points are simply immaterial at this stage, because all that you are trying to do is to persuade your prospect to contact you.

You will take care of everything else on the telephone with them. I hope you can see that, while this would not often be considered as part of the client conversion process, it is vital that it is covered here, to ensure that all your marketing is as effective as it can be.

The First Telephone Call

Once your prospect reaches the stage of contacting you, the client conversion process now properly kicks in.

There are three key parts to this process, but first let me talk you through a real telephone conversation that I had with a firm of solicitors when I was doing some mystery shopping for a client. You may find this very hard to believe when you read through it, but the following case study is a true story! I have not embellished it at all. It is recreated as it happened.

Reception found wanting

I was asked to call a firm that had four offices to enquire about a specific legal matter in which they were purported to be experts. I called the firm and was connected with their receptionist. I explained the matter that I needed help with and was met with this response: 'Who do you want to talk to?' and 'Can I have your reference number, please?'

I explained again that this was a new matter and therefore I did not have a reference number, and that as a new client I did not know who dealt with these types of legal matters, so I needed some guidance as to who could help me. 'So which office would you like to speak with, then?' was the Rottweiler's response.

How should I know?

I again told her which area of law my query related to but she still insisted that I choose one of their physical locations for my query. Playing her game (I am not sure that I would have carried on at this point if I was a genuine client but I was doing this for a client so I had to continue) I chose an office and was met with this response: 'That office does not deal with the area of law in which you are interested.'

By this point I was both laughing and screaming on the inside as this was such a poor client experience, but I also knew it was gold dust, as it would help me to persuade many other law firms to improve their client conversion procedures. I continued to play her game and plucked another of their offices from their website and was told that I was now in luck as they do deal with this type of enquiry. Obviously, however, it was not going to be all plain sailing now, was it?

'Which fee earner would you like to speak with?' was the next question from the angry lady.

I asked what my options were (please bear in mind that the term 'fee earner' should never be used in conversation with a prospective client – all it does is tell the client that all the solicitor is interested in is making money from them) and chose the partner rather than the solicitor. She then cut me off. I called back and when I explained what had happened, rather than receive an apology, I was greeted with this: 'Are you the man down in reception?' I explained again that, no, I was the man she had cut off, and this time she managed to put me through to the partner in question.

What a dreadful prospect experience. I guarantee that this woman is costing her firm tens of thousands if not hundreds of thousands of pounds in new fees every year by her appalling telephone manner.

Lessons to Learn

The case study experience was so bad on so many levels, and if I had been a real client I would have given up long before I reached the partner in question. You might look at this and think that this could never happen in your firm, but in my experience of calling hundreds of law firms, I can assure you that it happens more often than you could ever imagine. The main problems highlighted by this receptionist were

- the assumption that I was an existing client and should provide a reference number;
- the assumption that I would know which office I needed;
- the assumption that I would know which person I wanted to speak with about a new legal matter;
- the lack of knowledge of which offices handled the particular area of law I was interested in;
- cutting me off;
- referring to 'fee earners' rather than partners or solicitors;
- failing to identify the nature of my enquiry to the fee earner (partner); and
- a total lack of interest in my situation – or appreciation that I was someone who would be contributing to the payment of her salary in the future.

I can almost guarantee that some or all of these problems are happening in your office. So with this in mind, my next suggestion may not surprise you.

My strong advice is that all your marketing materials should carry a different telephone number from that of your usual office number, redirecting people to a call centre whose only job is to handle calls from new prospective clients for you.

This has several advantages:

1. The call centre will have more than one member of staff waiting to answer your telephone. Most law firms, if they do have a receptionist, allow the telephone to ring around to other

support staff if the receptionist does not answer within three or four rings. In my experience, everyone else goes out of their way to avoid answering the telephone so it often rings out. An outsourced call centre will solve this problem. Cost should not be an issue as they start from around £30 a month. The extra income from the clients who have been spared the receptionist ordeal outlined above will easily cover this cost.

2. It allows you to track the effectiveness of your marketing activities. You can insist that your call centre ask how the client found you, so you can see which of your marketing methods are working. When you ask your own staff to do this you will find that they tell you that the client cannot remember. It is funny, then, that when I ask a call centre to do this, they get the answer 99% of the time without any difficulty.

3. You can insist (and should do so) that your call centre fill in their own online enquiry form on your website for each new enquiry before transferring the call to your offices, which ensures that you can record your conversion rates as outlined above and have the relevant information in front of you when the call is transferred to you.

4. Your receptionist will be left free to deal exclusively with prospects and existing clients walking through your door, allowing him or her to give them proper attention instead of, as is often the case, answering the telephone in front of them leaving them waiting (which again is a common occurrence).

Your Receptionist

If you do continue to use your own 'Rottweiler' to answer new enquiries (also known as throwing money down the drain) I have a suggestion for you. Spend at least one day every month working in earshot of your reception desk. What you learn on this day could make you or save you thousands of pounds every year. Almost without exception your receptionist will be costing you new instructions, for any number of the reasons that I have encountered over the years:

- not answering the telephone quickly enough or at all;
- treating new clients inappropriately;
- failing to listen carefully to the nature of the enquiry;
- turning away clients with a legitimate enquiry because of a lack of understanding of the services you provide; and
- Failing to record accurately, or at all, how the client found you.

Please remember the point that I made at the start of this chapter: the whole purpose of all of your marketing is to make the telephone ring.

If, when your marketing is successful, the call is handled badly, or simply not answered, you have completely wasted the time and money spent on your marketing. You simply cannot afford to do this in the competitive legal services market in which you now operate.

Turning Away Clients

I want to home in on one of the points mentioned above: turning away clients whom you are unable to help or choose not to. I strongly believe that only a partner or office manager should have the authority to turn away prospective clients. There are two main reasons for this:

1. You will start to see trends. If you start receiving enquiries of a certain nature, you can make a decision about whether this is an area of law you should consider moving into. Moving into new or emerging areas of law can be very profitable.

2. If you have a lot of enquiries of a certain type, and you really cannot help the callers, you can refer them to another firm and can keep a log of all of the referrals made to that firm. If you find that you are referring several clients every month, you should set up a meeting to ensure that you receive reciprocal referrals. In most cases the other firm of solicitors will not be able to monitor the number of leads that you are sending to them, but if you do so you can show how important you are to their business and ensure that they reciprocate. (I go into this in more detail in Chapter 12.)

The Transfer

The next part of the client conversion process is about the fee earners who receive the phone call. The following are responses your receptionist or call centre will hear regularly when trying to 'hand on' a prospective client to a fee earner:

- 'I am just in the middle of something very urgent, can you get someone else to speak to them, please';
- 'I took the last call, isn't it Joe's turn'; or
- 'Ring-ring, ring-ring, ring-ring…'

Yes – the unanswered call, even when your receptionist knows that the person in question is at their desk! In the 'instant' world in which we now live, not dealing with a new enquiry as soon as it comes in is, in most cases, going to lead to the client going elsewhere.

Think about your own buying experiences. What do you do if you can't speak with someone when you are ready to take action? You will look for another supplier of the same service. Your clients are no different.

There are several solutions to this, depending on the size of your firm. In larger firms,

- have a new client team to deal with all new enquiries. Train them to take the matter as far as receiving the instructions and then hand over to a fee earner.
- allocate fee earners certain days of the week to handle new enquiries. Advise them not to do their most complicated legal work on those days, but to deal only with routine matters, so that they can break off at any time to handle a new enquiry.

In smaller firms,

- train a secretary or paralegal to handle all new enquiries – I have done this successfully. A solicitor does not have to deal with all new client enquiries; the first call is never about the law, despite what your fee earners may believe. The important part of the new enquiry is ensuring that you form a connection with the client (see The Meaningful Conversation below) and convince the client that you are the best firm to help them.

• you or a senior solicitor should handle all new enquiries.

The True Cost of Each New Enquiry

Often it is worth putting a value on the cost of each new enquiry generated so that all your staff realise why handling them efficiently is so important.

Use the formula below to work out the cost of every new enquiry:

> **Annual marketing spend ÷ new enquiries per month = cost per enquiry (advertising, sponsorship, brochures, website, website marketing, etc.)**

Even for a small high street law firm this is a good exercise to carry out. If we look at a firm turning over £500,000, with a marketing spend estimated at 5%, the example might be:

> **Marketing spend £25,000 ÷ new enquiries (per annum) 500 = cost per lead £50**

I find that when you attach a real monetary value to every telephone call, your team start to treat them more seriously and not ignore the telephone when it rings or make excuses as to why they cannot talk to a potential new client at that moment.

In the next section, we will look at the nature of the call, which is a vital part of the process.

The Meaningful Conversation

If your prospective client has made it past your receptionist (soon to be call centre, I hope), you have done well. We now move on to the crucial part of the process, and one that should not be rushed. This is where the only sales acronym you will ever need in your law firm comes into play: 2E1M

2E1M = Two Ears, One Mouth

Or, in its extended format:

Two Ears, One Mouth: Use them in the correct proportion.

If this part of the call goes well, subject to following up properly (by post) and not charging a disproportionate sum for your services, you will win the instruction. However, to win the instruction you must also remember this fact, which often confuses solicitors/ fee earners: the initial prospect telephone call is never about giving legal advice.

I know from many years' experience of training law firms that fee earners often dive straight into the legal issues because that is where they feel most comfortable and because they believe that will convince the client to instruct them. However, this rarely works.

So, if the meaningful conversation is not about giving legal advice, what is it about then? The meaningful conversation is all about finding out what matters to your client. Remember my marketing mantra: Clients First!

Understanding your client's needs and concerns is all that you should be looking to achieve in this call. If you can achieve this, you will have the best possible chance of winning the instruction. If you do as the other 99% of solicitors do and talk about yourself, your experience, you, you and more you, you will lose the instruction. The call must be all about your client, as a person, and what matters to them. This applies to both business and individual legal matters, because in both cases you are doing the same thing: selling your services to a person.

Let me give you some examples of telephone calls that I have heard and explain where the fee earner is going wrong.

1. Conveyancing call:

PROSPECT I would like a quote for moving house, please.
FEE EARNER How much is the house you are buying?
PROSPECT £300,000.

FEE EARNER OK, well, our legal fees will be £575 plus VAT, and the
disbursements will be xxx, xxx and xxx. How does that sound?

PROSPECT Well, I am just ringing round at the moment so I will
come back to you.

2. Personal injury call

PROSPECT I've had an accident at work, can you help me, please?

FEE EARNER Yes, I deal with lots of accident at work claims. I am
a member of the Law Society's personal injury panel and have
a lot of experience in this area. Tell me a bit about the accident.

PROSPECT I was going down a ladder and the rung gave way. I fell
20 feet to the ground, shattering my left heel.

FEE EARNER I am sorry to hear that [it's not genuine, as the solicitor is too excited that the prospect has a good claim – and
the prospect will be able to tell]. Yes, it sounds as if you have a
good case. When would you like to come in and see me so that
I can get the paperwork signed up?

PROSPECT I will have a think about it and come back to you.

3. Commercial call

PROSPECT Hi, I am in a partnership but we are unable to work
together any more. I want to discuss ending the partnership.
Can you help?

FEE EARNER Yes, I deal with a lot of partnership disputes. I
am something of an expert in this area. They can drag on for
months and usually cost a fortune, so the sooner we get started,
the better. When can you come in to see me?

I know that this is how most phone calls in all areas of law will
proceed. I have heard hundreds of them. You may be thinking
that these are quite normal phone calls and that that is how you
handle incoming enquiries. If you do think that, the good news
is that you are now going to learn a method that will increase
your conversion rates and make you more successful at securing

instructions, which will dramatically increase your profits without spending a penny.

The initial telephone call is all about listening. You must find out what matters to your client. Without this knowledge, how can you secure their trust and subsequent instructions? Remember, 2E1M means that if you are talking more than your client, you are failing in your task.

The call must be all about your client, their concerns, their needs, and what matters to them about the legal issue in question. They don't care if you have an urgent matter to attend to and need to rush them off the phone, or whether you want to get home early on the day that they call. Quite rightly, all they care about is feeling that they are being listened to and that someone who seems to care is showing some empathy about their situation. In the examples above, no one asked about the client.

In the first example, why was the client buying a house? Was it for themselves or a family? If they have a family or a spouse, are they relocating for a new job or a new school, which means that that timing is critical? How did they find the house? Is it the house they have been hoping to move into for the last five years and they cannot believe their luck that they are now going ahead? If the fee earner had taken the time to ask these questions, they might have found out what was important to the client. If they had, they would have built rapport and already started establishing a relationship with the client. They would win the instruction. This is what the meaningful conversation is all about.

People make decisions largely based on emotions. Think of all the times that you have engaged the services of others. I guarantee that on most occasions the person who won your business was the one who took the most time and showed a genuine interest in you. You must show a genuine interest in your prospects if you want to increase your conversion rates and win more instructions.

Before I dive into the details, I want you to hear from a solicitor who has already taken action. I think it will set the scene well for you.

75% conversion rate for conveyancing enquiries

Many years ago, I attended a conference on a mission for CPD points. The speaker was droning on and, even in those pre-smartphone days, the audience was finding ways to distract itself.

"You have heard all this before," said the speaker, breaking through the collective trance to be met with a general murmur of agreement, "but are you doing it? Knowing is not doing". I offer this brief case study in the same spirit. It is not original but it made a difference.

About three years ago I decided we would abandon all bulk referred conveyancing work and withdraw from all referral agreements. That meant turning away more than 20% of our turnover overnight. Instead we aligned our conveyancing service with the rest of the firm and looked for good quality clients paying a bit over the market average fees.

We started off using the same old approach:

"How much do you charge for conveyancing?"

"Well £x plus VAT and there will be disbursements including SDLT of £x, Land Registry of £x and search fees… "

"OK, thanks I'll get back to you."

Which of course they didn't, as another firm would undercut us. A large chunk of the market, tied to their referral networks, were not even ringing us for a quote.

We had to examine our process.

The first step was to take quoting away from the conveyancing team and done by someone who had the time to talk to enquirers without sounding as if they wanted to be doing something else.

Then we thought about what we were trying to tell the client; was it that conveyancing would cost them £x plus VAT or that we would look after them, talk to them when they rang and so on? How were we going to make the caller choose us? Could we really expect a client to compare solicitors on the basis of price and then choose the more expensive one?

That led us to the meaningful conversation.

We wanted callers to judge and compare us on the things that really mattered to them. For some that was the cheapest price, but for the majority, making the biggest financial commitment of their life, there were other issues. We found out those issues in the meaningful conversation, by listening to the client and asking questions so that we could understand what mattered to them and what was motivating them.

We have tried different ways and questions: timescales, reasons for moving, the type of property, location... We have even asked clients to consider what sort of a solicitor they wanted, "Ford or Mercedes", (and after reflecting overnight the particular caller chose us, representing the Mercedes).

The point is, we need clients to focus on what really matters to them and then form a judgment as to whether they think we can deliver that. For those who want a personal, proactive service, with experts in place solving and heading off problems, we were the right choice. For those who wanted the cheapest, we weren't.

A quality service offering is not the only approach and others would work – converted flat specialist, new-build specialist (and we also use that approach) – but whatever the proposition, we needed to understand where we could out-compete the opposition, understand what the caller wanted and then help them understand that we could deliver that.

Nick talks about people making decisions largely based on their emotions. That is undoubtedly true and for many we found the rapport the caller established with the person we had dealing with the enquiries was central to our success. Our person wasn't a fee-earner and in fact she has no legal experience. But she is intuitive, friendly, straightforward, listens and inspires confidence in her ability to deliver – or have the fee-earner deliver. Most importantly, she communicates at the caller's level, entirely free of the jargon or shorthand that the legal expert so readily deploys. The caller felt she was on their side.

Did it work? Our conversion rate fluctuates, depending on the competition and volume of transactions, but we see a conversion rate of 75% and better based on fees that are in the upper quartile. In other words, seven or eight out of ten callers choose us although we are more expensive (sometimes significantly more) than most of the competition. Our profit margin on conveyancing has more than trebled.

DAVID EDWARDS. BURT BRILL & CARDENS SOLICITORS.

Hopefully, that convinces you that this is a worthwhile exercise. Now, looking back to the examples above, let's see how they could be improved to make the conversations all about the prospective client.

1. 2E1M conveyancing call

PROSPECT I would like a quote for moving house, please.

FEE EARNER Certainly, Mr Hughes. Can I find out a little more about the reasons for your move, please, so that I can ensure I offer you the right service for your needs?

PROSPECT Yes, of course.

FEE EARNER Where are you moving from and to, and is there a reason for the move, such as a new school or employment?

PROSPECT Well, actually, I've got a new job and we're new to the area. I start my new position in eight weeks' time and we are in rented accommodation at the moment, which we need to be out of by then, too, so it is quite important that we move quickly.

FEE EARNER I understand. It's important that we can complete your move for you well in time for your new job. If we can agree the fees, how quickly can you have your mortgage in place, do you think? I want to ensure that that will not hold up matters for you.

PROSPECT Well, all of the paperwork went off to the building society this morning and they tell me that they should be able to get an offer out to me within seven days, subject to the survey results.

FEE EARNER That is excellent, Mr Hughes. We still don't have a lot of time, so if I can clear some time in my diary for you today, would you be able to come in so that I can start the ball rolling? Every day that passes could jeopardise your move date. I want to avoid that at all costs. When could you come in?

In this situation, by asking questions about the client's needs ('Clients First'), the solicitor has found the key trigger here – timing. He can now use that back in conversation with the client to show empathy. Your client may push for details of costs, but in my experience, they often will not if you have shown enough interest to secure their trust. You can discuss fees face to face when you have all the papers ready to go. If the client insists on hearing your costs on the telephone, by the time you present them, unlike all the other solicitors that they have called, you will be in a much stronger position to secure their instruction, having taken the time to find out what matters most to them.

2. 2E1M personal injury call

PROSPECT I've had an accident at work, can you help me, please?

FEE EARNER I'm sure I can, but to be certain can you let me know exactly what happened and how you would like me to help you, please?

PROSPECT Certainly. I was going down a ladder and the rung gave way. I fell 20 feet to the ground, shattering my left heel.

FEE EARNER I'm sorry to hear that. How are you now?

PROSPECT I'm still in hospital and in a lot of pain at the moment.

FEE EARNER I'm sure you are, Mr Hughes. How is your treatment going?

PROSPECT Slowly. I've got another week in hospital, and they are saying it could be as long as three months to recover. I can't afford to be off work for that long, as I won't be able to pay my mortgage.

FEE EARNER I can help you there, Mr Hughes, by obtaining a payment in advance of your compensation. This might ease the financial pressure for you and help you to pay your bills. Would that be helpful?

PROSPECT Yes, please, that would be really helpful.

FEE EARNER Good. OK, we need to move quickly then Mr Hughes. When can I come and visit you in hospital to get the ball rolling?

3. 2E1M commercial call

PROSPECT Hi, I'm in a partnership but we are unable to work together any more. I want to discuss ending the partnership. Can you help?

FEE EARNER Yes of course Mr Hughes. First, can you tell me a bit about your business and the challenges you are currently facing with your business partner, so that I can explain how I can help you?

PROSPECT We own and run a fishing lake. My business partner has lost interest in it and isn't helping at all, but still expects to take half of the income.

FEE EARNER I see. That does sound very unfair. What would be your ideal outcome, Mr Hughes?

PROSPECT Well, I love running the lake and want to continue to do so, so ideally I would like to be able to buy out my partner's share of the business.

FEE EARNER Excellent, I understand. In fact, I recently helped someone to reach an agreement with a partner in a very similar situation to yours, Mr Hughes. I was even able to put my client in touch with someone to provide the finance to buy out the other partner.

PROSPECT Really? That sounds excellent. When can I come to see you?

Notice the following in each of these calls:

- The call is all about the client and their needs, and not all about the legal issues. Using the client's name can sound clichéd, but it will always work. We are all very attached to our names, so you should use it, especially during the meaningful conversation.
- The fee earner, on discovering what the crux of the issue is for the prospective client, is able to suggest an action that excites the prospect and makes them want to get moving (the fast house move, the interim payment and the financing of the partnership deal). There will always be a trigger like this that you can draw out from your prospect in all of your meaningful conversations. It is your job to find this trigger.

I have some advice for you here: some fee earners, however hard you try or however much training you provide for them, will never be good at this part of the process. If that is the case, yet they are really good at the legal work, they should not handle the meaningful conversation. It is better to hand a matter over to them once the instruction has been received. I have instigated this in several firms where a fee earner is an expert in their field, but very poor at building rapport with the client.

Someone else, often a secretary or another solicitor, handles the meaningful conversation, secures the instruction, and then passes the matter over to the fee earner. How does this happen in practice? The call will go something like this: 'OK, our best conveyancer to get you moving as quickly as possible is one of our partners, Nick Jones. I'm pleased to say that you are in luck! I've just checked his diary and can see that he is free at 2 PM today, so we can get started straight away for you.' It is often easier to sing the praises of a colleague than it is to blow your own trumpet, so this works incredibly well.

Email Enquiries

I need to mention what you should do if the first enquiry from your client comes in by email or from a completed enquiry form on your website. Perhaps, more importantly, I need to mention what you must never do, under any circumstances:

> **You must never provide a quote for your services before having the meaningful conversation. Ever!**

If a client emails you or completes an enquiry form on your website, you should immediately call them back to have the meaningful conversation. If they have not provided a contact telephone number, you should send an email similar to this one:

Response to an email enquiry

Dear Mr Hughes,

Thank you for contacting my firm to ask if we can help you with your house move. I will be delighted to explain how we can help you and provide a price to do so, but first I need to find out a few more details from you.

If you can let me know which telephone number is the best one to reach you on, I will call you straight back. There is no charge, but it will allow me to discover all of the important details so that I can then provide you with a price to help you.

Yours…

Conveyancing is a good example here, as it is often seen as a price-only service, when it never actually is for all of the reasons that I have covered above. It is always about the connection that you form with your client. Let me show you what happens when someone makes the mistake of providing a price instantly, without having a meaningful conversation.

Missing out on the personal touch

A major national conveyancing provider dealt with a high volume of enquiries for their services and received a large number of instructions every month. To speed up the process, they decided to put an 'instant quotation calculator' on their website, meaning that they did not need to speak to prospective clients Now, instead of obtaining a prospective client's contact details and calling them back, the provider generated an instant quotation on the screen and an email confirming the quotation. Overnight, they stopped receiving instructions. Why?

The prospective client now had a price, but had not had a 'meaningful conversation.' They had no connection with the business in question, so when they spoke with the next business on their list, even if their fee was £50 or £100 more, the connection meant that that was the business that would receive the instruction. I hope this proves the point, because so many firms fail to grasp this.

You must have the meaningful conversation if you want to win the instruction.

If you send an email like the one above and the client just comes back and asks for a price, try again to explain that you can only provide a quotation when you find out more from them, and that this is too complicated to do by email but will take just a few moments on the telephone. If they will still not provide the details, I would still not provide a quotation by email, but explain again that until you have had a conversation with them, you cannot provide a price.

You may believe that you might as well provide the price, but I can assure you that in most cases you are not going to win the instruction this way, so I would persevere. It will pay you back in time.

The Follow-Up

Aside from the meaningful conversation, this part of the process is the one most likely to win you more instructions and put more profits into your firm's bank account than any other. I know this to be true, based on implementing hundreds of successful follow-up processes for law firms, so I am always staggered when I discover that most firms never follow up an enquiry for their services.

Let me remind you of my own survey figures:

- Always follow up   8%
- Sometimes follow up   17%
- Never follow up   75%

Please, I beg you, after reading this chapter, make sure you are in the 'Always follow up' category above. I promise you that it will pay back the very minor investment involved in setting up a follow-up process many, many times over.

Let's look at a client's experience with three different firms, and see if you can guess which firm is most likely to receive the instruction. The following chart goes through a prospect's experience when she contacts three different law firms. Which do you think looks more professional and will win the instruction?

Variable Follow-Up

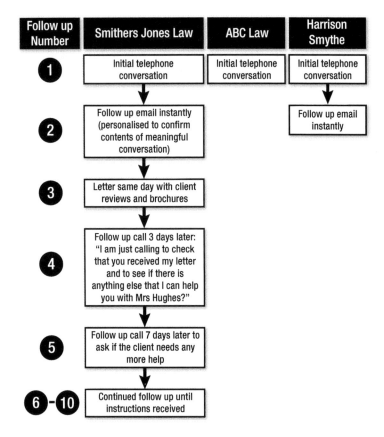

Follow up Number	Smithers Jones Law	ABC Law	Harrison Smythe
1	Initial telephone conversation	Initial telephone conversation	Initial telephone conversation
2	Follow up email instantly (personalised to confirm contents of meaningful conversation)		Follow up email instantly
3	Letter same day with client reviews and brochures		
4	Follow up call 3 days later: "I am just calling to check that you received my letter and to see if there is anything else that I can help you with Mrs Hughes?"		
5	Follow up call 7 days later to ask if the client needs any more help		
6-10	Continued follow up until instructions received		

Your client is choosing a professional service provider. The only impression they get of how professional and efficient you are before they instruct you is through your initial dealings with them. Which firm looks more professional in the image above?

Imagine what might happen if you get as far as having the meaningful conversation, which goes really well, but then you do nothing else. The prospect may be waiting for confirmation of all that was discussed, or, worse still they may fully intend to instruct you but then lose your contact details or forget which of the three firms they called is your firm.

If nothing comes in the post the next day (and, yes, it should be the next day), the opportunity is lost. That is another £50 to

£250 of your hard-earned marketing budget wasted. Remember that we are all different and have different needs and expectations. Some prospects will be happy with just a telephone call but others will expect (and need) you to follow up and confirm the outline of their conversation in writing. You must ensure that you cater to all requirements to ensure the best conversion rate possible. If you are thinking that an email is good enough; it isn't. So many emails find their way into junk or spam folders that there is simply no guarantee that your email will reach the recipient. A letter in the post definitely will, and will place you firmly ahead of your competitors in the professional service provider stakes.

Client capture is, in my opinion, more important than dealing with your current client matters. Without new clients, your practice has no future. Therefore, when courting new clients, you must show them how efficient you are. If you cannot 'dazzle' your clients with amazing service before they instruct you, why should they instruct you? This is your first chance to show this prospective new client how efficient and professional you are, so you really do have to send an email and a letter on the same day. Failing to take this follow-up step will reduce your conversion rate and will therefore cost you extra profits. For very little time and expense, this step will reward you many times over. You absolutely must follow up in writing for every call received, even if you cannot help the client on this occasion.

Here are follow-up letters for every occasion.

Follow-up letter – quotation/estimate

Dear Mrs Bloggs,

Re: Your {Purchase of Cherry Tree Cottage/Accident at Mick's Tyres/Your Purchase of your business partner's share of Fishy Fishing Lakes} *Make this all about what they are trying to achieve/the problem that they are trying to remove.*

Thank you for your call today. I really enjoyed speaking with you about *{repeat the nature of their enquiry again here/show that you understand their needs}.*

I will be delighted to help you with *{insert more details about their* *issue/matter}* and can confirm that your key concern is *{summarise what matters to them most here – e.g. to complete in 8 weeks before you start your new job/secure an interim payment to pay your mortgage/buy your partner out of your business as quickly as possible}.*

I confirm that I will *{repeat how you will help them with their issue/ legal matter – focusing on their need/pain}* and that my charges for this service are £XX *{try not to use legal terminology such as disbursements, or if you do, explain what these really are to the client – i.e. expenses}.*

I enclose my brochure which explains my services in more detail. I also enclose some recent reviews from clients who have already used my services.

All I need to be able to start to move things forward for you is *{spell out what they need to send back – make it as easy as possible using highlighter/stickers where they need to sign}.*

If you have any questions that I have not yet answered, please let me know immediately.

I look forward to hearing from you.

Yours sincerely,

Follow-up letter – unable to assist

Dear Mrs Bloggs,

> Re: {state nature of matter}

Thank you for contacting me today.

I am sorry that I am unable to help you on this occasion {Outline what, if anything, needs to change to mean that you could reconsider, or explain why you cannot help}.

I have pleasure enclosing a brochure which outlines my firms' legal services. If you or your friends or family need any help in the future, please do not hesitate to contact me.

Yours sincerely,

Obtaining the Follow-Up Address

I know that when I have introduced this process to firms in the past, one common 'excuse' is this: 'The client will not provide their address on a first call'.

This is simply not true. If you frame the question in the right way, 99 times out of every 100 your prospective clients will provide an address. They have called you because they have a legal need. You have taken the time to listen to their need, and explain that you can or cannot help them. At the end of the call you should say something along the lines of, 'If you can let me have your address I will pop a letter in the post to you so that you have everything in writing and my contact details if you need to come back to me for any more information.'

Who would refuse that request? If you are not taking the time to discover their needs, they might not see the reason, but now that you are having the meaningful conversation, this will no longer be the case.

Diary Note

Once the letter leaves your practice, a note should be entered into your diary for three days later, to follow up the enquiry with a telephone call if the instruction does not come in. When promoting legal services, it is much better to *serve* your clients than to *sell* to them. Therefore, if you enter the mind-set of serving a client, surely you want to call the client to ensure that they have safely received your letter and to see if they have any questions that remain unanswered?

This is all that you need to say: 'Hello, Mrs Jones, it's Nick from Smithers Jones Solicitors. I'm just calling to check that you received my letter in the post and to see if you have any questions that I can help you with?'

Remember, all you are asking is whether they have received the letter safely and have any unanswered questions. If they have received the letter and have no more questions, then quite naturally the next question is: 'Would you like us to help you with your [legal issue] then?'

If at this point if you do not gain the instruction, you can decide when to follow up again, and you should keep doing so until they tell you that they have gone elsewhere. Then you can ask why, so that you can make improvements to your process for the next time.

This is some of the most important work you can do to make your firm more successful.

In my experience of marketing law firms since 1991, both from the inside and the outside, building relationships is *the* most significant contribution you can make to improve the profitability of your law firm.

Following the 'meaningful conversation' approach

I believed that I was working hard on generating new work by using a variety of means including working with referral agencies and running a Google AdWords campaign. Despite this, our new business was stagnating. This was causing me real concern.

Within six months of implementing the 'meaningful conversation' approach and, crucially, the follow-up, I had doubled the number of new cases that we were generating each month, and within 18 months it was almost four times more. Admittedly, this increase was also down to other tools such as developing the website, however, I believe the follow-up process was the key to it all.

I find that tracking the leads as they come in is essential. Quite often, we do not manage to speak with prospective clients who have contacted us via our website until we have called them five, six, seven or more times. Before we introduced the systems, new leads were being passed to a fee earner who called them once, maybe twice, but then left it at that. This proved to be a huge mistake and was costing significant revenue that we had already spent money trying to generate.

PAUL DORAN, PAUL DORAN LAW.

The following chart of the entire process will help you implement it in your practice.

Converting enquiries

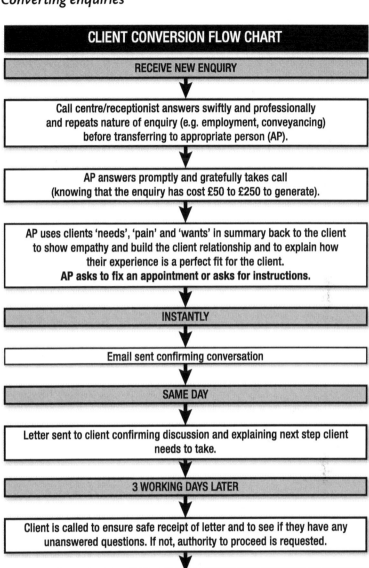

Chapter 6

DIY v DFY

My aim with this book is to set you free. I want you to be free from the idea that marketing is hard and that you cannot master it. I want you to realise and accept that marketing can and should be easy. It becomes a system much as drafting proceedings and issuing them, or exchange and completion of contracts.

If you follow the legal system of a conveyance, your clients end up in a new house. If you follow my system in this book, you will end up with a steady and consistent flow of new client instructions. It. Is. That. Simple.

It is that simple, that is, if you accept my system and don't fight it, which sadly I have seen too many solicitors do over the years, particularly when it comes to DIY v DFY: 'DIY' you should be familiar with – do it yourself; 'DFY' is 'done for you'.

When it comes to marketing your law firm, I promise you that the minute you accept DFY is the only way forward, you will start to attract a steady and consistent flow of new clients to your practice.

So why is it, then, that senior partners in a law firm so often tinker with their own website?

Why are they waiting to add that new page of content which they know should be on their website because it is such a core service offering of their firms, but constantly putting it off to 'manage their law firms', for which you can read 'firefighting'?

I cannot tell you how sad I am to have seen so many solicitors sabotage their own success by constantly trying to DIY, when, if they outsourced their marketing (DFY), everything would have been completed faster, more cost effectively and probably better – and, most importantly, it would actually have been done.

Instead, what happens, is that this senior partner convinces himself that he is the only person who can do this task of epic proportions. No one else can write the 400 words which will transform the success of his law firm overnight. So he waits. A week goes by, a month, a year, two years. Then one night he decides to do this task of epic proportions, but he can't quite make it as perfect as he would like, so he leaves it in draft format for another week, month and year.

Honestly. Stop it. Stop kidding yourself that you are the only person who can do that job. Someone out there is vastly more qualified to do it than you, and the best news is that the hourly rate that you have to pay them is significantly lower than your own hourly rate (which I hope isn't actually being charged any longer – see Chapter 15).

Let Go

You have to let go of control to be in control. This counter-intuitive statement is true. To be really in control of the growth of your law firm, by which I mean to see it growing consistently month after month, you actually have to relinquish control of it on a day-to-day basis. Your firm cannot wait for you to find the time to do what needs to be done to allow your firm to grow.

If you are trying to keep control of everything on a day-to-day basis, from the writing of content for your brochures to making changes on your website, and the managing of your Google Ad-Words campaign, the only thing that you are doing is not saving a few pounds in the short term, but in fact costing your firm hundreds of thousands of pounds in the long run.

Stop it. You can find someone to do everything that needs to be done right now, and for a maximum of £50 per hour, so why on earth would you try to do it yourself?

The excuses that I usually hear in this context are:

- I tried outsourcing once and had a dreadful experience; and
- No one can do it as well as I can.

I Tried Outsourcing Once and Had a Dreadful Experience

Did you meet your husband or wife or partner the very first time you had a date? Or did you, like most people, have to kiss a few frogs before you found your prince/princess? It is the same with outsourcing. You might not find a perfect fit to write your content, manage your Google AdWords campaign, or design your email marketing newsletter first time round, but such people do exist. You just have to keep looking until you find them. You might strike lucky and find them at the first time of asking, or it might take you two, three or four attempts, but you have to persevere.

As often happens in business, sometimes you can actually derail the process for the ridiculous reason that you want to prove yourself right: 'I will show that Jervis bloke that he doesn't know what he is talking about. I will outsource this project and when it all goes wrong I will be able to say "I told you so".'

You might think I am just being frivolous, but I promise you that I have seen this exact scenario play out many times. It is utterly bizarre when you think about it. The solicitor would rather go out of their way to try to prove me wrong than make more profits for themselves by building a bigger, better, stronger business. Remember, I don't benefit at all from a solicitor growing their business and making more money. I charge flat consultancy fees and the solicitor gets all of the financial benefits of attracting more clients every month after doing as I advise.

The saying 'You can lead a horse to water, but you can't make it drink' springs to mind, but for some mad reason I take a lot of pride in what I do. I gain my rewards in business not so much financially, but more from the success that my clients achieve.

I have two children in real life, but every one of my clients is like another child, or sibling, that I egg on every day that I work with them. I am desperate for them to grow and achieve the firm and the life that they deserve, so the self-sabotaging approach that they so often take to try to prove me wrong baffles me and wears me down.

So I am sharing this with you in the hope that you won't do this to yourself, but instead you will fight any natural urge to ignore me and accept that outsourcing all of your marketing so that it can happen 'with or without you' (WOWY marketing) is the only way to go.

No One Can Do It as Well as I Can

Even if you are right – and I am sorry to be the bearer of bad news, but you probably are not – it doesn't matter.

Remember, for your marketing to be hugely successful it has to have significant momentum, and one thing that is certain is that perfection kills momentum. Let go. Let someone else do a 'good enough' job and then when you have time one evening, go back and make it perfect.

You won't though; do you want to know why? Once you start letting go and outsourcing your marketing, your phone will start to ring more. More people will start to walk through your office door. More people will visit your website and more money will flow into your law firm. Once this starts to happen, you will kick yourself that you didn't outsource much sooner. Don't do that; just take pride in the fact that you have done it now and enjoy the new success of your firm.

As business owners, we are usually very good at criticising ourselves for poor or slow decision making, but not so good at praising ourselves when we do something right. Whether it takes you a few months or a few years; once you accept that someone else is more than capable of doing the jobs that you thought only you could do, enjoy the success that comes your way from that day forwards. You have earned it.

Chapter 7

The New Client Flowcast

Q How many methods of marketing does a solicitor need to produce a steady and consistent flow of new client instructions to allow them to reach their targets?

A Far fewer than you think. Two might be enough, but four is usually enough – if they are performed consistently.

Solicitors are usually surprised when I explain this. They often think they will need dozens of marketing methods to stand any chance of achieving their goals. It is often this belief that makes them think 'Why should I bother? I will just keep doing what I have always done and hope that it is enough to eke out a living.'

I have heard that exact response uttered with such feeling so many times. Life is simply too short to live in the hope that you can 'eke out' a living.

You can build a very good business with a great living if you just have two to four methods in place. My New Client Flowcast model makes this even easier for you by telling you which are the most important ones – your marketing arteries, in fact! I called them arteries because without them you are going to struggle, just as the human body would. However, put them in place and your working life becomes very much easier, much more profitable, and much more fun too.

Yes, you can have fun while running your law firm. It is allowed. In fact, I actively encourage it. Some of my best clients meet with me four times a year and after a good day of working on their businesses, we go out for a drink and a meal together with the sole aim of having some fun.

So, what is this New Client Flowcast, and why will it allow you to have more fun? I mentioned at the beginning of this book that my New Client Flowcast model is designed to show you how you can grow your law firm. Your firm and your profits are your blood flow, that is, the river in the diagram below, with the profits being fed by your marketing arteries and capillaries.

The arteries are effective marketing methods. These should be put in place first, as they are forms of 'peacock marketing' (of which more later) and can be set up to run with or without you, ensuring that your growth is steady and consistent, as opposed to up and down.

Let me put some meat on the bones for you, by naming each of the arteries and some of the capillaries – the lesser, complementary methods – that you might already be using in your firm.

The New Client Flowcast marketing model

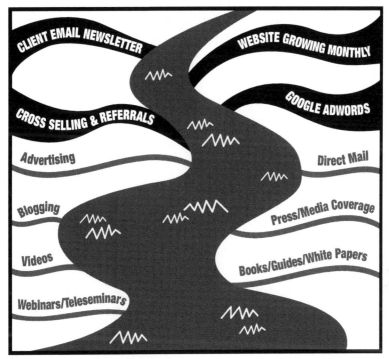

Key:

ARTERY - Put in place urgently

TRIBUTARY - Add after arteries

In the New Client Flowcast image above, the four marketing arteries are the most powerful forms of marketing for solicitors, based on many years of marketing law firms.

These are the ones that you really should have in place if you are serious about growing your law firm. They should be implemented and outsourced as soon as possible. Then all you need to do is to monitor them constantly and assess their performance, and ensure that your suppliers are making them work for you every month. If you have all four of these methods in place and working as well as they can (see Chapter 14), you will have a successful law firm.

If you have them all in place and have ensured that they are as finely tuned as is humanly possible to provide the maximum return on investment, then you can start to add some marketing capillaries into your marketing armoury and watch your law firm turnover and profits continue to grow.

I will explain all the marketing arteries in detail in the next few chapters.

Chapter 8

Your New Client Armoury

It is now time to look at the marketing tactics that will generate client instructions to produce the firm that you have always wanted.

You will remember from the New Client Flowcast diagram that not all marketing tactics are born equal. Some are much more effective than others. How do we know which are the real success stories and which are the also-rans? We can start with a simple test, which I call the 'peacock or elephant' test.

This is a visual reminder I provide for all my clients to cement the importance of making the right choice into their minds, so that they don't make the mistake of spending time and money on the wrong forms of marketing. I want to share it with you, too. It is a visual test that I want you to remember so that at 5 PM on a wet, cold, Friday afternoon in December when you receive that call from a salesman offering you the chance of a lifetime: an advertisement that will only cost you £1,000 if you say yes today, but which 'if you say no to will fall into the hands of your competition, leading your pathetic law firm to disappear into the ether...'

Yes, I know about those telephone calls. I used to get them all the time when I was practising. I used to enjoy playing the game, listening to the well-honed sales patter and then saying politely 'No, thank you, it is not for me but my competitor that you mentioned by name will, I am sure, be interested, so please do go ahead and sell it to them.' I would much rather they wasted their £1,000 than I waste my own.

I was never rude to these people; they were only doing their job. But wow, what a job!

The Two Forms of Marketing

There are two forms of marketing:

Peacocks	or	Elephants
Good	or	Bad
Attraction	or	Interruption

Let's talk about peacocks and elephants.

A peacock, when he wants to attract a mate, goes about it in a very charming manner. He fans his beautiful green, blue and gold tail and struts around in his glory. If a peahen is interested, she will let him know. It's subtle, gentle. A female who is interested approaches the male.

Now let's talk about elephants. Giant mammals! When they want a date, there is no beautiful tail to fan and no strutting to be done. Instead, the male elephant is a lot more forthright in his approach if he wants to mate.

He chases after the female and mates. That is pretty much it. She may or may not have much of a say in it.

What does this mean in the legal marketing world? What do peacocks and elephants have to do with winning more client instructions?

- With peacock marketing, you are putting your wares in front of your prospects at the exact moment that they are looking for a solicitor.

- With elephant marketing, you try and force your way into your prospects' minds regardless of whether they have expressed any interest in your services.

Which of these two methods do you think is going to be more effective?

If you can magically appear in front of your new clients at the precise moment that they are looking for you, will that be more effective than just appearing in front of thousands of people, the majority of whom do not need a solicitor at that time?

Which form of marketing do you think the sales representative is hard-selling to you at 5 PM on a wet, cold Friday afternoon in December? If his advertisement is that good, why does he have to sell it with a cold sales call? He is definitely selling you elephant marketing (also known as interruption marketing or bad marketing).

He is trying to persuade (force) you to buy some advertising in a pamphlet which may or may not be delivered to thousands of people who, more likely than not will never read it, and of those who do only a tiny number may have an interest in your services. Is that really going to work for you? No, of course not. This is why he has to use such underhand methods to sell the advertising to you: 'If you don't buy it, your competitors are going to buy it, and you will miss out and your firm will go down the tubes . . .'

Lovely – this type of marketing is to be avoided at all costs.

Let's look at some more marketing examples and see if you can work out which form of marketing each one is; peacocks or elephants.

1. An advertisement in the *Sunday Times* business section promoting your commercial services.
2. A billboard in your local town promoting your divorce services just after Christmas.
3. A Google AdWords advertisement for your commercial legal services appearing in the search results when a prospect Googles the term 'start-up business solicitor Guildford'.
4. Your firm being recommended to a prospect by one of your

regular referrers when asked if they can put them in touch with a solicitor.

Remember, the key question is this: 'Am I appearing before potential clients at the exact moment that they are looking for my services, or am I trying to force my way into their lives whether they have a need for my services or not?'

I will give you a moment to think these through; the answers are on the next page. (Don't look ahead, now):

1. *SUNDAY TIMES* BUSINESS SECTION ADVERTISEMENT: If you are appearing in the *Sunday Times* business section advertising your commercial legal services, you might say that you are in the right place. But, think about it for a moment. How many people reading that paper, on that Sunday, at that moment in time, are actively looking for a solicitor whilst dipping their soldier into their egg yolk?

The answer is absolutely none of them. Yes, one or two may need a solicitor soon, but it is a fraction of the people reading the business section, so this is definitely interruption/elephant/bad marketing. There are better places for you to spend your money.

2. A BILLBOARD PROMOTING YOUR DIVORCE SERVICES: The red herring here is that it is a local billboard, so I can see that some people might think this makes it good marketing. However, once again, the fact that most people passing the board will not need a divorce solicitor at that particular moment makes it interruption/elephant/bad marketing.

One point to consider here is that the cost may be relatively low, but nothing frustrates me more than the logic I hear so often used to justify this form of bad marketing: 'Well, at only £300 to place this advertisement, just one client and it pays for itself.'

Please don't use this logic. Yes, it may only be £300, but use this rationale 10 times a year (which I think is about the average based on the hundreds of solicitors I work with every year) and I can assure you that this £3,000 used on a peacock/ attraction marketing tactic will definitely give you a bigger return on investment (and a measurable one, at that).

3. GOOGLE ADWORDS: For those of you who do not know what this method of marketing is, or those of you who have tried it and failed to make it work, let me explain how it works.

Someone decides that they need something, some help or a product. They head to the world's largest search engine (currently – it will change one day but not yet) and they enter their search term into Google. For this example, let's say that they are a solicitor, like you, and they are looking for help to grow their law firm.

They type into Google the term 'solicitors marketing' and this is what they find in the search results.

Marketing Ideas For Solicitors – Solicitor (non-practising) UK
Ad 6 Fastest Ways For Solicitors To Attract Clients To Their Firm.▼
Contact Us For More Information.
Trusted By Solicitors UK Service Marketing For Solicitors

If a solicitor looking for help with marketing his or her law firm sees the offer to download a free book explaining the '6 Fastest Methods For Solicitors To Attract New Clients' what might they do?

I can tell you what a lot of them do: they click on my advertisement, download the book and then receive regular emails from me until sometime in the future they might ask me for some help. Now solicitors being a cautious bunch (understandably, bearing in mind how many of those late Friday December phone calls they receive selling interruption/elephant marketing) it is often a year or two before they ask me for help, but by then they know that I can help them.

The excellent news for you as a solicitor is that your clients are in need of your services far more quickly than my clients. My service takes time to understand, and needs a solicitor who is serious and committed to growing their law firm; your services usually provide a much more urgent fix to a far wider range of needs among the populace in general. If I am looking for a personal injury solicitor, it is probably because I am injured now – not because I am thinking about being injured in the future.

If I am looking for a 'business start-up solicitor, it is likely that I am looking to start a business now, not in 10 years' time. It is for this reason that Google AdWords is most definitely a form of peacock/attraction/good marketing. I will cover Google AdWords in more detail in Chapter 11. For now, please just let me assure you that if you are in the 'this form of marketing doesn't work for solicitors' camp, you are most certainly wrong. This is incredibly good news for you, because if that has been your view until now, you suddenly have one of the most effective forms of marketing for solicitors at your disposal, and I will show you how to use it.

4. RECOMMENDATION TO A PROSPECT BY ONE OF YOUR REGULAR REFERRERS: A referral from another business is deliberately a little trickier than the first three. I put it in to cloud the issue a little, but if you break it down, it should be clear which method of marketing we are talking about here.

We have a prospect who is in need of a solicitor right now. That prospect asks someone who already knows, likes and trusts you as a solicitor if they know any good solicitors who can help them with their needs right now. That referrer recommends you.

If we leave out the referrer, ultimately someone with an immediate need for legal help is being sent straight to you, so it is a peacock/attraction/good form of marketing.

I really want you to remember the peacock and elephant test whenever someone is trying to sell any form of marketing to you, because I know that over the years it can save you thousands of pounds of wasted marketing spend. I came up with this test because I became so frustrated when so many solicitors approached me having just spent hundreds or thousands of pounds on a form of marketing which I knew instantly would never produce any results for them.

I racked my brains for a visual image that would hopefully stick in their mind in the future so that when someone was making that pressurised sales call to them, they would quickly be able to assess whether it was likely to work for them or would simply lead them to throw their hard-earned marketing budget away.

Think peacocks not elephants!

The Marketing Arteries

Now we can move onto the marketing arteries in sufficient detail for you to understand what needs to be done to make them work, then how you can manage your outsourced suppliers by keeping tabs on crucial key performance indicators. Remember, my aim is for you to outsource all of your marketing so that you can continue to focus on growing your law firm. If you try to run your law firm *and* do all of the day-to-day marketing required, you will fail. You will hit a wall and not make the progress that you need to see.

We will look at each of the four marketing arteries in subsequent chapters, but before we do, there is one more very important thing you must do, which in my experience most firms do poorly or not at all: track all enquiries.

When it comes to marketing a law firm, every single marketing activity that you undertake *must* provide a return on investment for you. Nothing infuriates me more than hearing a solicitor say that they are doing something to 'build their brand'. Seriously? Brand building? If you are Coca Cola with millions to spend then maybe, but if you are a law firm turning over less than £10 million a year, you should never undertake any marketing that does not provide you with a return on investment.

So that you can ensure that each of your marketing arteries and capillaries is providing a return for you, you absolutely have to know how every new enquiry has been generated.

Tracking All Enquiries

Let me start with the common problems that I have seen when it comes to tracking new enquiries:

- Receptionists do not ask how people found you.
- Fee earners do not ask how people found you.
- Both of the above just classifying the enquiry as arising from a 'recommendation' because they forgot to ask on the call how the prospect found you and are far too busy and important (in their own minds) to call back to ask; or
- Law firm owners do not police this process.

Sorry about the last one, but if what I have said applies to you then it is a big part of the problem. If you are like most law firm owners, you spin a lot of plates. You try to keep on top of fee earning, billing, keeping clients happy, keeping the rest of the team happy, managing the finances etc. etc., so when you introduce a new idea or process, for example, asking people to track where all new leads come from, your team hear you say it, but they know that with so many other plates for you to keep spinning you will let this one drop, so they don't bother. They know that nine out of every ten of your ideas is a flash in the pan, because you simply don't have enough hours in the day to police them all (well, not before you read to the end of this book, anyway). Whether they do this consciously or subconsciously depends on the nature of the individual, but I promise you that this is what happens.

However, the good news is that the solution to this major problem is simple: you take the task away from them completely.

Call Centres

You outsource all new enquiries to a professional call centre and insist that they ask how people found you; because they are paid to do as they are told, they do it! You go from being completely blind and not really knowing how any of your new clients found your law firm to knowing how every single person that instructed you has found you.

This allows you to ensure that all of your marketing pennies and pounds are working for you. You can compile a summary table that might look something like this:

Marketing cost-effectiveness

Marketing activity	Cost per month	Clients generated	Estimated fees	Gross profit
Google AdWords	£1,000	10	£7,500	£6,500
Email marketing	£500 (content and software)	5	£3,750	£3,250
Referrals	£250 (lunch/gifts)	3	£2,250	£2,000

It will vary from month to month, but each activity must be in profit and – and you must be able to see that each one is in profit, otherwise how can you know whether you should keep it going?

The other point to remember is that the estimated fees are only those from the initial transaction. If you do your job well, these clients will not only come back and use your other services in the future, but they will also refer you to other people and businesses, because you will be keeping in touch with them regularly after reading this book.

I have a simple spreadsheet for you to use to start this process. Head to the resources section for the book, enter your email address and you will receive the spreadsheet for tracking new enquiries. www.samsonconsulting.co.uk/growth

The cost of engaging a call centre will be less than you think, but, more importantly, the ability to track with certainty how each new prospect found your firm will repay you many times over. Without this, it will be very hard for you to grow your firm in line with your aspirations. I am happy to recommend a call centre. Simply ask me for some details. They work with a number of my clients (as well as handling all of my enquiries too).

Procedures for tracking

Once you have signed up with a call centre, this is the process that I recommend that you have them follow:

1. A new enquiry comes in to the call centre.
2. The call centre asks how the new prospect found you.
   - For online enquiries, they will ask for the exact search term (it will be in front of your prospect on the screen at the time of the call, so this is not difficult and will be answered in 90% of cases, whereas most legal receptionists will say it is impossible to obtain this information – it really isn't!).
   - If the prospect saw an advertisement, they should be asked the name and date of the publication;
   - If the prospect received a recommendation or referral, they

should be asked the name of the person who recommended them; or

- If the prospect received one of your emails, they should be asked the date of it.

3. The call centre handles the enquiry and completes a form on your website that is for their unique use. This must be separate from your usual website enquiry form, so that you can track which leads they are handling and ensure that they are providing value for you.

4. When they click 'send' on the form it will be emailed to your firm instantly, so that it can be up in front of the person to whom the call is transferred.

5. The caller will be transferred straight to the person handling the new enquiry. I strongly recommend that the call is transferred immediately. Taking messages and asking someone to call the prospect back will lead to delay, which will lead to many of the prospects going to find another solicitor. This instant world needs instant answers.

6. You convert a new client and know exactly how they found you!

Now that you are tracking every new lead into your practice and know exactly what led to your prospect picking up the telephone or filling in the enquiry form on your website, let's get some more people heading your way, shall we?

Let's look at the most powerful marketing tactics for law firms first – your marketing arteries – before moving on to your capillaries. I have put these arteries in order from one to four for a reason, so if you do not have any of them in place, start at one and work your way down the list implementing them.

Chapter 9

Marketing Artery 1: Your Existing Clients (Email Marketing)

There is one piece of advice that I wish I had been given when I started my consultancy in 2003, which is this: 'Start your email list today on Day One of your business, Nick.' I imagine that my response would have been similar to yours when you were starting your business: 'But I don't have any clients yet, so there is no point in starting an email database/list.'

I would have missed the point completely, as do so many business owners and, more importantly for you, so many solicitors. If you do not yet have an email marketing database, start it today. Add one person to it. Now you have a live email marketing list and can start adding to it every time you speak with any prospect, client or referrer about working with you.

Before you know it, you will have a database of thousands of prospects and clients. When you have that it means that you can write an email (have an email written for you), press the 'send' button and communicate with a few thousand people instantly. Imagine that just one of those people had a need for your services at that moment. Wouldn't they be highly likely to instruct you, rather than be shopping around just on price? Yes, is the answer, in case you were wondering.

So many solicitors spend so much time talking about starting an email database but never get it off the ground because they believe that they first must compile a list of everyone who has been in touch with them over the course of the last few years, and so they put it off. Soon another six months has gone by, and then a year, and still there is no email database in place.

What a waste of opportunity! It takes seconds to start an email marketing database.

Indefinite delay

I once worked with a firm who were determined to obtain every email from their database before they started their email list. They thought they had several thousand emails available, so they waited until the list was finished. Some years later they still had no email list because they hadn't completed the task.

That represented years of wasted opportunity of growing their practice the easy way. Years of lost revenue. Hundreds of clients going elsewhere for legal services because the firm failed to contact them and remind them that they existed.

The sad truth is that even if they had managed to compile the list, most of the emails would have been out of date, and, because most good email marketing providers require 'double opt-in' (see later in this section), only about 20% of all people on the database would have actually made their way onto the email list.

You are far better starting your email list today and adding to it slowly but surely. This way, as you will be adding people while they are live prospects, they are much more likely to accept your invitation.

There are countless email marketing providers in existence. I can strongly recommend the one that I use, and I will even provide you with a free video showing you exactly how to get started as part of the resources that accompany this book. Head straight to www.samsonconsulting.co.uk/growth to find out more.

Whoever you speak with from this day on, add them to this list. You will soon have a substantial email marketing list. It is that simple, so please do it. Remember, this is your first marketing artery, because it is one of the most important – and certainly one of the cheapest – methods for selling more of your services. Sending one email a month to your email marketing list leads to an increase in recommendations and referrals, often a substantial increase.

It is such a worthwhile exercise and an incredibly cost-effective one, too. Aside from the low cost of the software, a few hundred pounds buys you the content that you need for your email newsletter, which also feeds Artery 2 (adding unique content to your website). Cost effective and effective. Worthwhile? I hope you will see that it is.

Setting Up Your System

Now, if I have persuaded you that this is the right thing to do, how are you going to make a start?

1. What is double opt-in?
2. Can you send the emails yourself or do you really need the software?
3. What type of content should you prepare?
4. How much content should you prepare?
5. How often should you send your email newsletter?

Double Opt-In

First, let's get rid of some technical language for you: double opt-in. A good email marketing software provider asks anyone who agrees to go onto your email list to confirm their email address before they are added. This serves two purposes:

- it ensures that the email address that they have provided is genuine; and
- it confirms that they have asked to be added to the list.

It is this double opt-in process that ensures the email software provider is able consistently to deliver 99% or more of your emails to your recipients. If you skip this process or go with an email provider that does not offer double opt-in, then, though you may not realise it, very few of your emails will ever be delivered. Your objective of trying to win business from this exercise will never be achieved if no one receives your emails.

I have heard many so-called marketing experts say over the years that double opt-in is a bad thing, as many people will be omitted because they didn't see the first email or refuse to click the link. However, this is to miss the point. You want the people on your email database to receive your email, because you want them to instruct you; if they don't receive your email, what chance do you have of being successful? None. Double opt-in is a good thing. Yes, some people will slip through the net and not make it onto your database, but those who do click the link in the email and get added to your email list will receive your emails in their inbox every month, which increases the chances of you receiving referrals and recommendations.

Using Your Own Email Software

In case you are thinking that you can simply compile an Excel spreadsheet of all of your clients, prospects and referrers and do an email merge from there, please completely disregard that as an option.

Your emails will not reach anyone. You will have a cap placed on the volume of emails you can send at any one time, and you will soon exceed that, meaning that your emails will simply never be delivered.

For the sake of around £20 a month, the double opt-in email

marketing software that I recommend is the best option in terms of security and deliverability.

What Type of Content Should You Prepare?

I recommend the following email marketing template, which gives you some flexibility but not so much that it stops you ever putting an email together in the first place.

- Introduction
- Article 1
  - Headline, introductory paragraph, and a link to the full article on your website
- Article 2
  - Headline, introductory paragraph, and a link to the full article on your website
- Closing notes
- A call to action, including a link to your main services on your website, which will remind them of all of the ways that you can help them.

Remember that the main purpose of your email newsletter is twofold:

1. to remind people that you exist and keep your firm's name in the front of their minds; and
2. to sell more of your services.

It is vital, therefore, that each time you get in touch with your clients and prospects you include a link to all of your services, and a call to action. Here is how the email might look in practice.

Email newsletter

	From ▼	njervis@samsonconsulting.co.uk
▣	To...	
Send	Cc...	
	Bcc...	
	Subject	What your business needs to know about copyright

Dear Nick,

It seems to have been a busier month for many businesses in and around Reading. We have helped more start-ups to launch than at any time in the last 12 months, and with a new business park given planning permission this month it seems that this trend will continue.

The property housing market is also busier than it has been for some time.

As always, if you need any help, please do ask us.

Business Copyright
Did you hear about the local business owner who has just been fined several thousand pounds for breach of a competitor's copyright? We have examined what happened and what you can do to ensure that you do not make the same mistakes.

Click here to read the full article:>>

How Long Does It Take To Move Home?
There is often a lot of negative press about moving house, so we thought it might be worth exploring what happens when you move home and show you how you can make the process go more swiftly.

Click here to read the full article:>>

Need Some Help?
Please remember that we are here to help you with all of your legal needs, including:

- Business services
- Conveyancing
- Employment
- Family
- Probate & Trusts
- Wills

Simply reply to this email or call us on 01234 567890 and we will be delighted to help you.

Kind Regards,

John Smithers

Some firms become fixated with adding logos and images, but these are simply not necessary, bearing in mind the two objectives above. You are aiming to keep your name in front of your clients and prospects, and to win new business. Adding your logo and images actually threatens both of these objectives. First, most images are automatically stripped out of your emails by the email software used by your prospects, and second, if the first thing a prospect sees when they open your email is your logo, they instantly know that you are selling to them. This makes it highly unlikely that they will read your email, meaning that all of your efforts have been wasted.

If you make your email look like one of your normal emails to someone, as above, there is a far greater chance of it being read, and a far greater chance of it achieving its objective, namely, making your telephone ring.

I strongly recommend that you follow this formula to start with. The good news is that it makes it much easier for you to prepare and send your emails (or, even, to outsource that process).

Subject Lines

When it comes to email marketing, the most important part of each email is the subject line. If you do not make any effort to make it work for you, you will miss some great opportunities to win new enquiries quickly from your emails. Although I state later in this chapter that your open rate (i.e. the percentage of people you send your email to who actually open it) is not something to fret too much about, you do want to give yourself the best chance of people reading your emails, so spending some time ensuring that your email subject line is engaging is a good idea.

Let me start with some dreadful email subject lines based on ones that I have seen in my inbox, and then I will give you 50 ideas to get you started and to use as inspiration when you are checking through your monthly email before sending it.

BAD SUBJECT LINE 1: **The Smithers Jones Email Newsletter.** Why bad? Because it contains the firm's name and what it is – in other words, telling the recipient that they are being sold to. It would be the equivalent of Amazon sending an email with the subject line 'Buy some more stuff from us.'

BAD SUBJECT LINE 2: **Our monthly email.** As above.

BAD SUBJECT LINE 3: ... Yes, blank. I have received quite a few like that over the years.

Suggestions for Email Newsletter Subject Lines

Here are 50 suggestions for you which I hope you will use each time you check over your email newsletter before hitting the 'send' button – or preferably asking your supplier to hit the 'send' button.

1. How to...
2. Why does...?
3. What this says about...
4. Do you know how...?
5. Seven questions to ask before...
6. Ten reasons why...
7. Don't do X before...
8. Complimentary guide shows you... [I use 'complimentary' as 'free' often puts your email into the spam folder]
9. What this story can teach you about...
10. Why I chose the law
11. Why your business needs to...
12. Your Will is out of date...
13. Is there really a compensation culture?
14. How to dismiss an employee correctly
15. Have you ever thought about this?
16. Don't always believe what the insurers tell you
17. Are your employee contracts up to date?
18. Sale Now On [dare you?]
19. 101 reasons why you should never...
20. Is the cheapest always the best?
21. Make your Will online for virtually nothing
22. How the cheapest Will cost the most
23. How he moved home without an estate agent
24. What is a settlement agreement?
25. Can I exchange and complete on the same day?
26. Was my dismissal fair?
27. Should I lease or buy commercial premises?
28. As featured in the *Maidenhead Advertiser*...
29. Did you see this in the news?

30. Is the UK really the whiplash capital of Europe?
31. What is a Shareholders' Agreement and do I need one?
32. Will this rain stop for long enough to ... ?
33. Why I stopped reading the business newspapers
34. Have you ever tried this for your business?
35. Have you ever tried this?
36. How many solicitors does it take to ... ?
37. If you get what you pay for, can I pay more please?
38. What to watch out for when buying a new car
39. Shopping and your retail rights
40. What is medical negligence?
41. What is clinical negligence?
42. The changing legal services market and what it means for you
43. DIY Divorce, should you?
44. How to avoid care home fees
45. How to care for my elderly parents
46. What is probate?
47. Financial settlement during a divorce
48. Who will get custody of the children?
49. Is this discrimination?
50. Did you hear about the solicitor who ... ?

The Content

Who Should Write It?

The purpose of your content is to make your prospects think about the variety of your services, not to explore the detail of the legal process. I see so many firms completely miss this point, particularly if they ask their own solicitors to prepare the content for their website and email marketing. Generally, in my 25+ years' experience, solicitors are good at being solicitors but fairly hopeless at anything else whatsoever!

It is one of the reasons why you should have your content 'done for you' as opposed to trying to 'do it yourself' (see Chapter 6). The other reason is the cost and hassle it will save you. The cost saving is clear, in that your solicitors should be charged out at hundreds of pounds per hour, whereas your copywriter shouldn't exceed around £50 per hour.

The hassle saving is perhaps even more important, though, in that if you ask your solicitors to write the content for you, not only will it be full of legal jargon and usually terminally dull, but you will also have to chase them time and time again because it is simply not a priority for them.

This is why you really should outsource your copywriting to a copywriter.

Style of Content

We have established that the purpose of your content is to make your recipients think about the services that you provide and perhaps, more importantly, about why they should use them as soon as possible.

All your prospects care about when they read your emails is how the content relates to them. If it doesn't relate to them at all, most of them won't read it. You will have the odd person who finds all of your emails fascinating, but the truth is that the majority will only read on if the topic relates to them. This is why I recommend the format above, with a couple of different main topics so that you have twice the chance of appealing to your recipients.

Let's have a look at how this might work in practice with a few different examples.

Rights and Wrongs of Newsletter Content

Target audience	Law firm content	Copywriter content
An elderly unmarried woman with children	**Inheritance tax** We specialise in providing inheritance tax advice and have done so since 1932.	**Have you made every effort to reduce your inheritance tax bill?** Whilst tax avoidance is illegal, there are steps that you can take to reduce the inheritance tax payable on your estate for the benefit of your loved ones.
A married father of two	**Make a will now.** If you don't yet have a Will you really should make one now!	**Have you properly protected your children?** Did you know that 73% of fathers have failed to protect their children in the event of a serious illness or injury?
A female entrepreneur	**Business Contracts** It is important to have contracts to protect your business. We have been preparing contracts for businesses since 1971.	**Is your business growing as quickly as you would like?** It is often easy to get carried away with the excitement of running a business without taking the time to stand back and see if your business is growing in line with your expectations, and perhaps more importantly your needs.

Your job is to get your prospects reading and then to make them take action at the end of the article if the content relates to them. You will never achieve this objective if your headlines and opening content are strictly legal.

In the second column, I've set out how the content might appear from a law firm that doesn't understand what they are trying to achieve in each of the situations; it's just starting from the position of the services that it wants to sell to the recipients. The content in the third column talks directly to the prospect about the position they are in at this moment in time. It will strike a chord with those reading the email. I hope you see the point that I am making.

Of course, both have the same goal in mind, but if you can't persuade your prospects to read the email in the first place because it is clear that you are only trying to sell your services to them, there is virtually no point in sending it.

I will go into more detail about the remainder of the content, including providing a content writing template, in the next section, which is about your website. Remember your email should not include all of the content, just the headline and the opening paragraph, and then an invitation to your recipients to click through to your website to read the rest.

Adding People to Your Database

Importing Existing Clients and Prospects

All software providers have the ability for you to import subscribers to your email marketing database from an Excel spreadsheet or similar, so if you have a list of email addresses for clients already, then it is worth doing this.

However, remember the two points that I have made about this:

- Don't wait until you have updated your spreadsheet with all of the clients that you know you have somewhere in your basement to start your email list. Just start today with what you have.
- Only about 20% of those you import initially will make their way onto your database through the double opt-in process. Why is this figure so low? Because you are adding them to your database some time after they have originally been a client, so they might not remember you or they might decide they don't want to receive emails from you; 20% is still better than 0%, so it is worth doing.

When you import this list your software provider will ask how you obtained these contact details. It is important that you comply with any legal requirements, so whilst at the time of writing this you are allowed to email your clients on non-matter-related topics as long as there is an unsubscribe button on each email (there is – another reason why you must use email software providers), you must satisfy yourself legally that everyone on the list is a client.

This is another reason why you might only consider adding people from the day you start your email database as opposed to importing old contacts, although if it was my firm I would take the chance that even 20% of say 1,000 is 200 people worth having on my list, but as I say, you have to be satisfied that you are being legally compliant. You are the solicitor, after all.

Adding People After the Initial Import

Once you have established your email database and carried out your initial import of clients, how do you add more people to it? Perhaps I should start with how not to add people to your email list.

Don't have a form on your website that says, 'Sign up to our newsletter'. Why?

Ask yourself if that puts your Clients First? No – it simply says to them that you want their email address so that you can keep telling them about your services. While this is true, you can perhaps see now that it isn't very appealing from the client's perspective.

You have to be much more proactive in this process of adding people to your email marketing database, and this is the formula that I suggest you follow:

- Add a form to a page on your website that is primarily for you and your team to use. I suggest you put it on a page that is easy to find, for example www.yourdomainname.co.uk/email. That way you will remember how to find it. The email marketing software provider will provide you with the form for your website.
- When you are on the phone with any new prospect, an existing client who is not yet on your database, or a referrer, add their name and email address to that form on your website. I advise that you don't even mention that you are doing this. Remember, the double opt-in process means that as soon as you add them to your software they will receive an email from you asking them to confirm their email address. If you were on the phone with a potential new service provider and you received an email from them during the call, wouldn't you be impressed at their efficiency and simply click the link in the email to confirm your email address?

That's it. A simple process to add new people to your email database.

If they are already on your list from the initial import, you don't need to worry about them being added twice. You will simply see a message after you submit the form that states that you already have an entry for them on your database.

Autoresponder Emails

Most email software has the ability to provide automatic follow-up emails once someone adds themselves to your email marketing database. For your main client/prospect/referral email database I suggest that the first automatic email simply says hello and is relatively informal.

However, the beauty of all email marketing software is that you can have more than one database, so you can create different databases for different types of services.

This might be helpful if you sell a service that is that is often not needed instantly, for example, a business start-up or business sales service, because someone might research starting their business long before they actually pluck up the courage to get going. Therefore, if they find your website but do not yet need you to help with their start-up you can offer them a free legal guide to business start-ups and then automatically schedule the software to send a sequence of emails at intervals chosen by you.

The sequence might look something like this.

- Day 1: Send the free guide offered.
- Day 7: Offer a free telephone discussion about starting a business.
- Day 21: Expand on part of the information contained in the free guide.
- Day 49: Expand on another point from the free guide.
- Day 77: Expand on another point...

You get the idea. Each email is written once, but then will be sent to everyone who downloads your free guide from your website. In each of the emails you can sign off by offering a free telephone consultation when they are ready to start their business.

Email software packages all handle this process slightly differently, but they all come with video training. The main point is that you simply create a new email database –in the example above this might be a business start-up database – then you create a form offering the free guide, add the code to your website, plumb in the automatic follow-up emails, and you are up and running.

I know I've urged you to outsource your marketing, so you will actually be getting someone else to do this for you, but I just wanted to stress that it is very simple, even though it is one of the most automated forms of marketing that you can create for your firm.

This is the same process I use with solicitors. I sell a service that is rarely required instantly, so I offer a free guide entitled *The 6 Fastest Ways for Solicitors to Win New Clients*, then I send a few emails offering a free telephone consultation called the 'More Clients Now' strategy call. If they don't take me up on my offer initially, after around 42 days they are moved over to my general email marketing database, and then they will hear from me once a week.

If you bear in mind that most of my best clients had been on my email marketing list for around two years before they start working with me, you can perhaps see why I said at the beginning of this section that I wish I had started my email marketing list earlier! However, this slow drip system only works for services without an instant need for help. If you sell conveyancing, personal injury, employment or family services your best bet is to sell the free initial enquiry from your website and all of your marketing, because your prospects have an instant need that you can help them with.

I will go into more detail about this in the next chapter but for now please trust me on this. I have tried the free guide method for all types of legal services and it really only works for services that it takes some time for prospects to commission.

Business is the obvious legal service for two reasons:

- Existing businesses usually already have a solicitor and only go looking for a new one when their current one has upset or frustrated them. They may not be ready to change just yet, but if you offer them something of value in exchange for their email

address and keep in touch with them, when they next fall out
with their solicitor you will be at the front of the queue.

- Start-up businesses often spend some time researching and
thinking about starting up before they actually do it. Again,
being able to keep in touch with them right up to the time that
they are ready to get going is vital if you want to create a steady
and consistent flow of new client instructions.

Frequency of Emails

How often should you keep in touch with the prospects and clients
on your email database? Every month, as a minimum. How do I
know? I have tested emailing less frequently, and I can tell you that
you will miss too many opportunities to win new instructions. If
your emails are really good you could even send them fortnightly
or weekly (see the section on optimisation later in the book), but
I would start with monthly.

Let me address some of the common fears here, in case they
are starting to run through your head.

Q But people will get annoyed if I email them once a month?

A There is an unsubscribe button on every email. Some people
will use it from time to time. That is fine. If you aren't annoying
anyone with your marketing *ever* it is a sure sign that you are
not doing enough of it!

Q What on earth am I going to say every month?

A That really shouldn't be your problem. That is what you will be
hiring a copywriter for. The truth is that once you get used to
the idea, you will start having your own ideas about topics that
could be covered. You will start seeing headlines in the paper
or local stories and think of a legal angle to them. You can ask
your copywriter to cover these.

I have sent an email nearly every week since 2003, when I started my marketing consultancy. I promise you that when I started I
found it a lot harder than I do now. If you had asked me then if I
thought I would still be coming up with ideas for my emails 13 or

14 years later, I would have considered you a crazy dufus with fluff for brains. However, now that I have done it I can tell you that it is actually much worse for me if I don't write my emails. They are good for me – and I hope for my clients and prospects too. Judging by the many kind responses I receive, they seem to work well for them too.

People unsubscribe from time to time, but that is all part of the process. Usually they are solicitors who have consumed all of my free information and attended many of my webinars but never taken any action, so they would never be a good client for me anyway. My clients have to take action, otherwise I have to let them go. I gain my job satisfaction from my clients' successes, so if they are not doing anything it really isn't working for them or for me.

Consistency of Emails

If you do not consistently send emails to the people on your database this marketing approach will not work. Consistency is the lifeblood of an email marketing newsletter. Without it, you might as well not bother. It is another reason why outsourcing your email marketing newsletter is so vital, because then all you need to do is to check that it was sent when it was supposed to be sent.

You need to put a diary note in stone to send your email newsletter on or around the same date each month, for example, the first Tuesday of every month, or the last Thursday. If you do not do this I can assure you that before you know it three months will have passed without you sending an email newsletter. Then, when you do send it, those on your email database wonder what it is about because they haven't heard from you for some time.

Ensure you send your email newsletter consistently if you would like it to deliver new clients to you on a regular basis.

Your Key Performance Indicators

You now have the software and the email formula, so what do you do next? Your job in this entire process, remember, is simply to monitor your statistics every month to ensure that your email marketing campaign is achieving its objective, which is to generate more referrals and recommendations. Of course, you can only know this if you check your statistics. Let's look at the figures that you need to track each month.

YOUR SUBSCRIBERS: This is the total number of people receiving your emails. Obviously, this number should rise dramatically at first and then at a more leisurely pace, but it must continue to rise. If it isn't rising, that tells you instantly that you or your team are failing to add people to your email database.

YOUR OPEN RATE: People can become fixated on this number, but you really shouldn't. Yes, in an ideal world 100% of the people on your email database would open your email every time you sent it, but that is simply not going to happen. Generally, if you hit 15–25% you are in the 'average' ball park (whatever that is).

But it isn't so much about open rates. I have had people on my email database not open an email for months, but when they needed help they opened it, read it, and suddenly got in touch with me and became a client.

The widespread advice in the ether from many so-called 'marketing experts' is every so often to clear out people who have not opened an email from you for a few months, but if I had followed this advice it would have harmed my business. I strongly recommend that you do not delete people from your email list simply because they have not opened one of your emails for a few weeks or months. They could become one of your best clients as long as your firm's name keeps popping up in front of them, but delete them and you have no chance of this happening.

If you need any more persuading that it is not all about open rates, please consider your own email habits. No doubt you receive emails from Amazon, Tesco or other providers. I bet you don't open every single one that they send to you, but I also bet that when you want to buy something online you remember where to go.

You need to be in the same position with your legal services. You need everyone on your email list to think of your firm when they next need a solicitor or when someone asks them if they can recommend a solicitor. That only happens when they keep seeing your email in their inbox even if they don't open it. So please don't become fixated on open rates, nor on the following click-through rates.

YOUR CLICK-THROUGH RATE: Your click-through rate is the number of people who click from your email onto your website by following the link to your articles. You want to see some action here, but again it is not something to become fixated on. It can range from a very low percentage to 30% if your content is right for your audience. It will rarely be above 50% so, as I say, please do not fret about it.

THE DATE SENT: IT is important to keep track of the day that each email was sent as it will ensure that you tick the 'consistency' box, which is vital. You can send your email on the first Thursday, the second Tuesday or whenever you prefer, but make it about the same time each month for maximum impact.

YOUR RECOMMENDATIONS AND REFERRALS: This is the most crucial number, is it not? After all, this is what we are trying to achieve: an increase in referrals and recommendations as a result of a consistent and engaging email marketing campaign.

Therefore, it is imperative that you track and record all of the recommendations and referrals that you see every month. There is nothing more motivational than seeing your hard work producing results, so when you see your recommendations and referrals rising each month you will know that it has all been worthwhile.

Use the spreadsheet that I referred to in Chapter 8 so that you can see the trends in this area month after month. You should start to see a steady increase within three months of beginning this process, with your maximum impact achieved at around 12 months.

—

You now have all that you need to start your firm's email marketing database and newsletter.

If you do not already have one in place, start it today and you will soon begin to see results in the form of new instructions.

Chapter 10

Marketing Artery 2: Your Website

I might have started with your website, but more likely than not you already have one of those. Instead, I wanted to ensure that you started your email marketing newsletter database first, so that by the time you finish this section you could already have 50 people on it to start communicating with.

Which would make now the right time to talk about your website.

I love websites for law firms – not in the sense of finding them gorgeous, inspirational, exciting things, but because when they are built properly, they can generate new clients for law firms on a consistent basis. The sad news for me, though, is that in all viewing of law firm websites – and I do far too much of it to be healthy – I rarely find good ones.

I might find websites that look stunningly beautiful because the website design company has persuaded the unsuspecting solicitor that this is a good idea, while failing to mention that it won't in fact make the telephone ring. Or I might find other websites that follow the latest trends, for example, an 'infinity' website, where all of the content is on one page and you scroll forever to read it; again, these do not produce new clients for their law firm owners. What I fail to find, though, are websites that do the only thing that they are supposed to do: produce new client instructions on a consistent basis.

The cruel part of this is that whether a website produces clients or not has virtually nothing to do with the amount of money that is spent on it, but much more to do with whether it follows the basic rules for a client-generating website. I have seen websites that cost £1,000 to set up produce hundreds of thousands of pounds' worth of new client instructions each year, while other websites costing £25,000 or more never deliver one single client instruction. I cannot tell you how much this frustrates me, so my aim in this chapter is to ensure that you never make the mistake of owning a useless law firm website. I want to set out what your website must do, what it mustn't do and give you all of the tools required to ensure that your website ticks all the boxes. I will give you everything that you need to ensure you have the best website possible.

Why should you listen to me on this topic? Well, I think I am particularly well qualified when it comes to knowing what makes a law firm website work. I have spent hundreds of thousands of pounds of my own money generating clients for law firms through my own legal service websites, and I have worked with hundreds of law firms to ensure that their websites do the same. Everything that I share with you is based on tried and tested marketing tactics.

So I ask you to forget everything that you have read about websites before now, or everything that your website developer or designer has told you (usually they have no idea at all, by the way – more of that in a moment), and read the next few pages with a completely open mind. If you do this, I guarantee you will be much better placed to understand what you need your website to look like in order for it to produce clients for you. If you are just about to embark on updating your website, or even better, if you are a start-up firm and are about to create your first website, following this formula is going to make your life so much easier and your law firm website so much more successful.

Let's look at some fundamentals of what your website should and should not do before I put the whole thing together into a foolproof checklist to ensure you do not make any of the common mistakes.

Your Website Should Never Sell Your Legal Services

That sounds rather counter-intuitive, doesn't it, especially when these words are coming from a law firm marketing specialist? Surely that is the whole point of a website.

Yes and no. The website will deliver clients to you, but the purpose of the website is to make your telephone ring, or encourage a prospect to complete your enquiry form or email you, rather than to try to sell your entire service.

So many firms fail to grasp this and feel that they must sell every aspect of their legal services from the pages of their website, so they go into great detail about their services and how to instruct them, often even including a Word document that a prospect must complete before they will even speak with them. Really? Good luck with that. It means that you will instantly lose 50–75% of the enquiries that otherwise might come your way.

Remember, your job is to put your Clients First, and make their lives easier not harder. If you do need a Word document completed before you can act for them, fill it in for them once you have won their instruction. If you need certain pieces of information from them, get them from the first telephone call, once you have listened to their needs and convinced them that you are the right firm for them.

If you take away every potential barrier to a client making contact with you, your website will be fit for purpose. If a client visits your website and is presented with detailed forms or questionnaires to complete, but then goes to your competitor's website where they are asked simply to make a phone call or fill in their details to make contact, which are they going to do? In this instant world, your competitor will receive the enquiry.

If you currently make it too difficult for your prospects to get in touch with you from your website because you are trying to sell your full service, you need to simplify your website. Make it clear that you have the expertise that your prospects are looking for, but then explain that all that they need to do to find out more is to fill in an online enquiry form or call you.

That is it. Your website has done its job if this is all you ask your clients to do.

Prices

The second key point is that you should never put your prices on your website. Once you display your prices on your website you will rarely be contacted by any potential clients, because you have now put yourself in the position of being a price comparison website. Unless you really are the cheapest law firm on the planet for the service in question – and I urge you never to be that because you won't survive long or have a fun, profitable law firm – then you simply become the yardstick prospects use when they call other solicitors to enquire about their services.

I must mention at this point the price comparison websites for legal services which seem to be popping up these days. It is my strong advice that you do not touch them. They are designed to present a price to the end user and therefore the only way that the end user (your potential client) can determine who is right for their needs is with price. Price is never a good way to sell any service, let alone a professional service.

If you get your own website in order and market it properly, as explained in this section and the next one, you should find that you gain more than enough clients to help you hit your targets. If you are looking at these price comparison websites as a quick fix, which is something I hear a lot from solicitors, you can get faster and more cost-effective results by fixing your own website now.

I see so many firms constantly chasing quick fixes to generate new client instructions yet never spending any time on their own marketing arteries or capillaries (see the New Client Flowcast in Chapter 7). If you have a severe cut on your arm or your leg, you know that the only way to stop the bleeding is to have it stitched. Plasters might buy you a bit of time, but at some point, you need to get to hospital and have the wound cleaned and stitched. It is the same with making your own website work versus buying in clients from other people's websites. It might work for a little while, but unless you make your own website work properly, at some point your business is going to need to go to hospital. Don't leave it so long that infection has set in and it can no longer be saved . . .

Automated quotations

Do you remember the major provider of conveyancing services I mentioned earlier, who used to invite prospects to enter a few basic details and then call them back with a price. This worked well for years, but then someone decided to automate the process and provide an instant quotation once the prospect clicked 'send' on the quotation form. Overnight, they stopped receiving instructions. Why?

They had become a price comparison website: once people saw how much they charged they could call the next provider on their list and say: 'We have been quoted £575 by Smithers Jones Conveyancing [not their real name, of course]; how much will you do it for?' Now the new firm knew the price they had to beat so they just dropped their price to beat the quote, meaning that Smithers Jones didn't receive any telephone calls or instructions.

Smithers Jones quickly went back to their old system.

I hope you can see now why displaying your pricing structure on your website is not a sensible thing to do. All you need to do is to stress that the first call or enquiry is without charge or obligation, then when you have had your meaningful conversation with the prospect you can discuss pricing. There is more advice on pricing later in the book too – advice that will enable you to sell more services at a better price, so it is well worth a read.

Every Page of Your Website Must...

... tell your prospect exactly what you expect them to do when they reach the end of it. Never assume that your prospect will trudge off and find your telephone number on your contact page. Even if you have your phone number at the top right of every page (a wise thing to do), please do not assume that your prospect will scroll back to the top of the page to find it.

'Clients First', remember. Make it easy for them. Tell them your phone number at the bottom of every page, include your email address and a link through to your free enquiry form (of which more later). You have to spell out exactly what you expect your client to do at the end of every page. If you don't, you will lose opportunities to win instructions.

Think about the statistics that you are working with here: on average a client will now usually only visit one to two pages of a website before making a decision to get in touch. Have I just plucked this figure from the air? I wish I had, because then it wouldn't be such a startling figure, but sadly not. This is based on the dozens of law firm websites that I work with. Google Analytics (see later in this chapter) shows me exactly how many pages people visit on each site.

You must bear this in mind when you are working on your website. If your average visitor is only going to look at one or two pages of your website, however beautifully crafted it is and however wonderful the words each page, do you really want to make them hunt around for your contact details? No, of course not. You want them to read enough quality content for them to realise that you are the firm of experts that they need for their particular legal issue. The second they reach that decision, they need to be able to find your contact details instantly, hence the need to include your call to action on every page, sometimes more than once if it is a particularly long page.

Call to Action

What should this call to action say? Let's look first at how it might appear at the bottom of your page.

Website Call to Action

Make a Free Enquiry

Call us now on 01234 56789, email **info@smithersjones.co.uk** or complete our **Free Online Enquiry** [*links to your enquiry form page*] for a free, no-obligation discussion and let us explain your legal rights and options.

Some solicitors are terribly scared of the word 'free', but you shouldn't be. Remember that the only purpose of your website is to make your prospect contact you. On the flip side of this equation, what is the one thing that prospects are still terrified of when speaking with a solicitor? Yes, cost. Therefore, you have to do something to take away this fear. Please remember, you are encouraging them to 'make a free enquiry', you are not promising them free legal advice for life. When they call with you, listen to their needs, explain how your service matches them (this is the meaningful conversation), and then tell them what the next step is. That is it.

In my experience, adding the word 'free' to your call to action makes your telephone ring. Now that you are fully trained in the art of turning a prospect into a new client, if your telephone rings more you will generate more client instructions. It really is that simple, so I strongly suggest you test this out by using the word 'free' in your call to action if you are not already doing so, at the bottom of every page.

If you don't currently have a call to action at the end of every page, it is well worth adding one as quickly as possible, as it will lead to more instructions for you.

The Two-Minute Trust Builder

I mentioned in the preceding section that you only have one or two pages to persuade your prospects that you are the right legal experts for them and that they should get in touch with you.

I have some more bad news for you. You also have less than 120 seconds to convince them of your expertise – 120 seconds or less (I am seeing this number decreasing universally across law firm websites) to convince someone that you are the *only* solicitor for their needs right now. That's less than two minutes to prove beyond any doubt that you are experts and that they should – must – make contact with you.

How do you do this? You use my two-minute trust builder system. I spent a lot of time and carried out an awful lot of research to create this system, because I realised that it was vitally important if my Marketing4Solicitors members were to have websites that worked as hard as possible to create more clients for them.

I looked at all the concerns a prospect might have when choosing a solicitor and then devised a framework to ensure that they were all so clearly visible on every page of the website that the prospect could not miss them, even if they did only spend two minutes on the website and looked at only two pages.

There are two elements required to convey your expertise to your prospects in under two minutes:

- depth of expertise
- proof of expertise

Depth of Expertise

Imagine you sold fruit, but rather than selling all fruit, you decided to be a specialist in apples. If I walked into your shop and only found one type of apple on the shelf, would I really believe that you were an apple specialist, or just someone selling apples? With only one type of apple, it would be the latter, so you would have failed to convince me of your expertise.

It is exactly the same with your legal services. If you are to persuade me that you are an expert – and in this day and age you absolutely must do this because 'average solicitors' are ten a penny – then you have to have sufficient content about each of your legal services to convince me that this is the case.

It never ceases to amaze me when I speak with a solicitor on a 'more clients now' strategy call and they tell me that they cannot understand why they never receive any enquiries from their website. I take a look with them and find one page for each of the services that they provide. One page of content. Really? Does that convey expertise? Not in a million years. In fact, it simply conveys laziness. You need to convince me that you are an expert; one page is simply never going to do this.

Shrinking website

I once created for a firm a website with dozens of pages for each service that they provided. Within a few months it was generating an awful lot of enquiries. I stopped working with them some time later, but met up with one of the partners a few years on. In the process of catching up he seemed quite excited to tell me that they had replaced the monstrous website that I had created for them with a very simple five-page website.

I replied, 'Oh wow, and overnight your telephone stopped ringing too, yes?'

'How did you know?' was his reply.

I wasn't gleeful, just sad that they had replaced a website that worked with one that didn't. There were a lot of pages on their website because they served two purposes:

- The number of pages gave Google and other search engines more chance of finding my client's website and putting them in search results for the services that they provided; and
- The depth of content once someone arrived at their website proved beyond any doubt that they were experts in the area of law in question.

> Once these pages were removed, however, Google had several hundred fewer chances of sending visitors to the website, and when someone managed against the odds to stumble across their website, there was no way they could, with only a handful of pages, convey sufficient expertise to encourage the prospect to call them. A sad tale. Please don't make the same mistake for your firm.

Everything I do has a reason for it, as I hope you are beginning to understand. I don't just make things up. I try them and I test them. I check the results and then try to improve on them, all with one simple purpose: to make my clients' telephones ring more; to make them busier to make them more profitable; to allow them to enjoy their law firm and their life more.

So, what does a website with enough pages to convey expertise on a given matter look like? This is the family law section of the website of one of my long-term clients:

If you count them, there are 13 pages relating to family law, including the main page. Most law firms have one page for each service. Who looks more like an expert if you are the prospect?

Remember the process: when the prospect starts searching for a solicitor, they will land straight inside this family law section (because that is where Google will send them on the basis of the volume of pages in this section), and instantly they can see 13 pages all relating to family law. Surely this firm must do a reasonable amount of this type of legal work to have written all of these pages about it? What else can the prospect think?

When they find the next firm's website with just one page about family law, what will they think of that firm?

The truth is, however, that they won't bother going to another website. This website ticks all the boxes so they will make contact and as long as the solicitors do a good job of converting the enquiry into a new client the prospect will have found their specialist family lawyer.

Ideally you want a minimum of 10 pages for each legal service that you provide. Any less than this and you're not really trying. Now if you are thinking that you provide 10 different services, so that means at least 100 pages and that's too much like hard work, it really isn't. You can pay a copywriter to do it for you. (I can recommend one, so just ask me.) Also, you don't have to do them all at once, you could set a target of 2 to 4 a month

When you get to this point, you will find another wonderful thing happens: more and more people will find your website and make contact with you. Why? Google will love all these extra pages and will send more people to your website – as long, that is, as you have enough words on each page, so let's take a look at that now.

Content Per Page

How many words should you put on all these pages now that you have them? Anything from 400 words to 2,000 words.

Surely no one can write 2,000 words about a legal service without sending someone to sleep, can they? Yes, they can. A good copywriter can, and as long as you follow my content-writing checklist later on in this section for each page on your website, it is much easier than you would imagine.

The reason you need so much content is two-fold:

- to ensure Google knows exactly what this page on your website is all about, so that it can send more people looking for help to it; and
- to provide enough information to persuade the people who arrive on your page that you are legal experts in this area and to make contact with you.

There are of course many other search engines out there, but the only meaningful one at the time of writing this book is Google. It will change in time, but for now Google is king, and all the other search engines play by similar rules anyway, so let's look at what they are trying to do.

The sole purpose of a search engine is to find answers to the questions that people are typing in to them. How does Google assess all of the billions of websites that exist online? It sends its little automated website readers, called 'spiders', to go and read them all (crawl them) and report back to the Google Master on what they found.

If one of these little 'spiders' reads a page on your website with 25 words on it, what can it say when it reports back to the Google Master? The following translation from binary code gives an approximation of how this conversation might go!

GOOGLE MASTER Spider 399, tell me what you found when you visited the website named Smithers Jones.co.uk and tell me now, boy!

SPIDER 399 Well master, I am not really sure, if I am honest. I found the word 'solicitor' once, the year 1899, and the word 'specialists', but that is about it, really. I don't really understand it myself, although I am sure it must mean something to them.

GOOGLE MASTER Very well, then. Let's not bother putting them in our search results. If they don't know what they do, how on

earth should we? Our customers don't want that sort of non-
sense being presented to them, do they, 399?

SPIDER 399   I agree, Master. Sorry for wasting your valuable time.
I will try to find a better website on my next visit.'

I have been to Google and I can assure you that this is exactly
what happens – well, I like to think so as it makes it a lot more
fun. Google does indeed send its spiders to read every page on
your website, and if there are no words, or very few, on a page, it
simply doesn't know what the page is about, so it either will not
list that page in the search results, or if it does it will be below
hundreds or thousands of other pages on other websites so will
never be found.

To give Google a chance of knowing what your page is about,
you have to have a minimum of 400 words on each page, but ideally
between 750 and 2,000. This way, the spider can pick up the essence
of what the page is about, and it gives you a real chance of being
listed higher in the search engine results than your competitors,
particularly if you have lots of these pages in existence for each
legal service because you have followed the advice above.

Once you have all these lovely pages with all these lovely words
on them, if you structure 'behind the scenes' correctly, you stand
a really good chance of attracting more prospects to your website.

Behind the Scenes

There is information that Google's spiders read that you might not
even know exists. I need to make sure you understand it is there
and show you how to find it so that you can see if it is being used
properly on your website. This is dull, technical information, but
it is important so I need you to bear with me even if you are not
technically inclined. Remember, my purpose is to show you what
you need to know but you then need to get someone else to do
the legwork for you.

These techy bits are called 'meta' tags and titles. I think it is
easiest if I show you an example. Here is the 'behind the scenes'
code from my own website home page:

```
<title>Legal Marketing Services | Marketing For Solicitors</title>
<meta name="description" content="Marketing For Solicitors Specialist!
Need Legal Marketing Services Help To Win You New Clients? Samson
Consulting - Marketing For Solicitors Made Easy."/>
```

How can you see your hidden code? Easy. Go to a page on your website in your preferred browser, then somewhere in the middle of the page (not on an image, but on some words) right click on your mouse and select 'View Page Source'. You will then be presented with a page of what is technically known as 'gobbledygook'.

The easiest way to find your way around this page of gobbledygook is to press CTRL F (find) to search the page and then type in the phrase or code you are looking for. This saves an awful lot of time and will allow you to see if your website people are doing their job properly (beware, generally, they are not).

First, search for the word 'title 'to find your title tag. This is the title for the page. It is really important, yet sadly on most law firm websites that I review it is either not completed or, even worse, the same wording – usually the law firm's name – is used on every page of the website. This is a huge wasted opportunity.

Let's go back to Google Spider 399. When he comes to your website, he doesn't read the page that your website visitors see. He reads the 'behind the scenes' code that makes your page come to life. He is a techy, so he soaks up all of that code to find out what the page is all about. The first thing that he comes to is what you see above; the 'title' tag and 'description' tag (the 'keyword' tag is not so important now).

These tell Spider 399 what your page is all about before he even reads anything else on the page. Perhaps, even more importantly, the 'title' tag and the 'description' tag are the exact words that will appear in the search results if your website is successful and makes its way into the top few results of Google's search. The accuracy of these words is important to Spider 399 but also for enabling prospects to find your website. This is your chance to attract someone to your website. You mustn't waste it.

Let me show you what I mean, by showing you how my website page is presented in the search results.

Legal Marketing Services | Marketing For Solicitors
https://www.samsonconsulting.co.uk/ ▼
Marketing For Solicitors Specialist! Need Legal Marketing Services Help To Win You New Clients? Samson Consulting – **Marketing For Solicitors** Made Easy.

The same words from my 'behind the scenes' title and description tags become my 'advertisement copy', as it were, which will hopefully persuade a solicitor to click through to my website. You might have noticed that I use leading capitals in both my title tags and description tags: if it stands out more, it is more likely to be clicked on by a prospect. I have tested this comprehensively when using Google AdWords (of which more later), and I advise you to do the same.

Therefore, your title tag, description tag and keyword tag must tell Spider 399 what your page is all about. Let me give you a legal example. Let's say that you are a business solicitor providing employment law services to employers. On the page in question for this example, you are aiming to generate unfair dismissal instructions. This is how your tags might look:

Title: Facing An Unfair Dismissal Tribunal Claim?

Description: Are You An Employer Facing An Unfair Dismissal Claim From A Disgruntled Employee? Read On To Discover The Best Way To End The Claim.

Keyword: unfair dismissal tribunal claim

You will notice that the key phrase, contained in the keyword section 'unfair dismissal tribunal claim', is included in all three tags, which is really important if you want Spider 399 to send back a good report about this page back to the Google Master.

The next piece of code that is important is your 'H1' tag, which is the next thing Spider 399 is going to look at. This is actually the title of the page that your website visitor will also see, and it should be exactly the same as your title tag above. Sometimes, website designers don't use this in the way it is intended, so you might find your 'H2' tag is the heading on the page that your visitors see. If this is the case, ask them to change it. It matters.

After the 'H1' tag, Spider 399 does then read the page in the same order as your prospects. The first paragraph after the 'H1' tag should also include the keywords that you are featuring on the page to give you the best chance of Spider 399 reporting back favourably.

After that, you are safe to freestyle, save for the fact that any images on the page should also be 'tagged' to tell the Spider what they are showing (he sees the world in code and words, not pictures, bless). Let's carry on by using the example of my home page, on which you will find my mugshot (my mother likes it – sometimes).

```
{caption id="attachment_2288" align="alignright" width="174"]<img
class="wp-image-2288 size-medium" alt="Legal Marketing Services Spe-
cialist Nick Jervis" title="Legal Marketing Services Specialist Nick
Jervis" src="https://www.samsonconsulting.co.uk/wp-content/up-
loads/2015/07/cricket-website-174x300.jpg" width= "174" height="300"
/> <em>Nick Jervis<br />Solicitor, non-practising and cricket
fan</em>[/caption]
```

You will notice, because I have underlined them, that the same words appear in the 'alt' tag and the 'title' tag. This is because different browsers read these tags slightly differently. Google reads the 'title' tag, whereas Internet Explorer/Edge reads the 'alt' tag. If you don't have them both, you will upset some of the major browsers and miss opportunities.

You now know the behind-the-scenes coding that you need to be able to check. It may be a bit dull, but I would be doing you a disservice if I didn't go through it with you, because it is so important for giving you the best opportunity of allowing more prospects to find your website.

Now you should have an understanding of how to convey sufficient depth of expertise in terms of volumes of pages and volume of content on each page, plus how to code behind the scenes to make the most of it, you need to provide proof of your expertise.

Proof of Expertise

Once you have established depth of expertise and attracted people to your website, how do you then convince them on these one or two pages and in under two minutes that you really are an expert?

This is what you need:

- Testimonials/Reviews
- Case studies
- Qualifications
- Press coverage
- Number of people helped

TESTIMONIALS/REVIEWS: When you buy something on Amazon, do you read any reviews before you make a purchase? Thinking of buying a new product or gadget? Read the review. A new book to make your business better? Read the reviews. (By the way, if you are finding this book helpful, as I sincerely hope you are, please do leave a review, thank you.)

People are now used to reviews and expect to find them. Therefore, I think the time is right to start using this terminology in the legal world, too. Have a reviews page rather than a testimonials page, which, let's face it, is not a very user-friendly term.

More important than what they're called is where they are: you should have reviews clearly visible on every single page of your website. Remember, your visitor will only see one or two pages, so it is important that they see a favourable review on every page. The ideal place is on the right-hand side of the page, which is what I call the 'proof of expertise' column. Here is a snapshot of how it might look from my website 'wireframe' (which is the main outline/shape/style I recommend for your website).

Website wireframe

LOGO plus "Solicitors" plus strapline explaining why your prospects should choose you

REASON WHY?
One sentence/paragraph

TELEPHONE 01234 567890
EMAIL info@smithersjones.co.uk

TOP NAVIGATION (to most common pages) eg. Home | Services | About Us | Free Enquiry | Contact

LEFT NAVIGATION	CENTRAL CONTENT	CONVERSION COLUMN
Makes it easy to travel around your website whilst reading your content.	Using this width for content makes it legible. If it covered the full width of the page, as many websites do, it becomes illegible.	**FREE ENQUIRY FORM** Short form or button linking to free enquiry form page.

LEFT NAVIGATION
Makes it easy to travel around your website whilst reading your content.

For example:
> Home
> Conveyancing
> > Buying
> > Remortgaging
> > Selling
> Probate
> Wills

Note: conveyancing navigation opens to reveal inside pages when inside that section.

Include address on left side below navigation if you provide local services.

If national services, include a map showing which areas you cover.

CENTRAL CONTENT
Using this width for content makes it legible. If it covered the full width of the page, as many websites do, it becomes illegible.

HEADING
Subheading

CONTENT Minimum 400 words if you would like people to find this page (not necessary on contact page but for all main services pages it is).

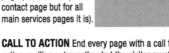

CALL TO ACTION End every page with a call to action spelling out exactly what the visitor must do next.

CONVERSION COLUMN

FREE ENQUIRY FORM
Short form or button linking to free enquiry form page.

Please enter your details below to make a free enquiry

Name
Email
Telephone
Brief nature of enquiry:

Send Free Enquiry

REVIEWS BOX Includes one testimonial with an option to "Read more" to be taken to the reviews page.

PROOF OF EXPERTISE Include logos of specialist qualification/press coverage etc from the "two minute trust builder".

I like the option of the testimonial/review changing on each page, but also giving the user the opportunity to click a left or right arrow to change the review that they are seeing, along with a link to 'read more reviews', which takes them to a page full of them.

This is a key point. How many reviews do you need to collect? 6? 10? 50? 1,000,000? If you reach the last number, you could probably think about slowing down your collection process, but why would you stop before then?

Let's go back to the reason why we are collecting reviews in the first place, which is to provide proof of your expertise to a visitor so that they make contact with you.

If your visitor sees 6 reviews, which is probably all they will see on your competitors' websites, they might be satisfied. However, anyone can collect 6 reviews. If your visitor sees 100, 1,000 or 1,000,000 reviews, wouldn't they be utterly convinced by the overwhelming evidence that you really are experts? At that point, will they want to call a firm with 6 reviews? I don't think so. They will want you because you are clearly the best, so you receive the call, not your competitors.

If reviews are so important, why do so few firms have more than a dozen? I believe that this happens for two reasons;

- they don't understand the value of many reviews (you do now that you are reading this); and
- they don't have a system for collecting them regularly.

Everything needs a system. The purpose of this book is to teach you my tried and tested systems for generating clients for law firms. The simplest system for collecting reviews is this one:

> CLIENT Nick, I cannot thank you enough for the work you have done on my legal matter. I am so grateful.
>
> NICK Thank you so much, that is lovely to hear. Would you mind popping that in an email to me, please? It would be really helpful for other people like you who are considering using my services.

If they agree, you can even make it easier for them by putting what they have just said into an email for them and simply asking them to approve it, so that you can use it on your website and in your printed marketing materials.

The other way to do this is to send an end-of-matter questionnaire to clients just *before* the conclusion of their matter, asking for their feedback and including a review box. The timing is crucial. If you send it to them after they have moved house, received their settlement cheque or started their business, then you will be lucky to hear from them. However, send it to them when they still need you to do something for them and it dramatically increases your chances of them sending it back to you.

Note: I once talked through this process in an email to my database of solicitors and got an irate response from one of them, saying I was encouraging her to fabricate reviews. I read and re-read the content of my email, which said nothing of the sort. It said, as outlined above, that if someone gives you great feedback, ask them to put it in a review for you. You have to receive the feedback or ask for it first; you can't simply make it up. I thought I would put that in here for the sake of clarity, as I know you legal guys and gals can be sticklers for detail.

CASE STUDIES: While reviews are important in the 'two-minute trust builder' process, case studies can take things to a completely new level. This is because they dive deeper into the reasons for someone deciding to instruct you, what happened when they did, and the results they achieved. If a prospect in a similar position reads their case study, the fact that you have previously helped someone just like them to achieve a successful outcome makes it far more likely that they will instruct you.

You should go out of your way to generate case studies. The way to create them is to turn your best reviews into case studies. The clients who go out of their way to provide you with a wonderful review will be happy to take it to the next level and allow you to put more information into a case study, which can then be rounded off beautifully with their review at the end. In my opinion you should always ask the client to sign off your use of the case study on your website. Most of the time they will want it to be anonymous, but that is fine. The words will still speak volumes. If they are happy for you to add their name, even better, but the content of the case study is what will help prove your expertise to your prospects.

At the end of each case study I would be inclined to add the following: 'Smithers Jones would like to thank [the client/name] for allowing us to publish their story above.' This shows prospects that if they do decide to instruct you, you won't publish their story without their permission.

Case studies can be presented in the righthand conversion column or interspersed with the content on the page related to the legal service in question.

QUALIFICATIONS: I see a lot of firms including specialist qualifications on their websites, which pleases me immensely. Sadly, however, they usually do so in the worst possible way, which defeats the whole point.

Let me explain what I mean. Suppose I start looking for a probate solicitor and I find one who proudly displays the STEP logo (Society of Trust and Estate Practitioners), the relevant qualification. However, as a member of the public, I haven't a clue what this really means but I surmise that it might be important as it is so prominently displayed on the page. I click the logo and, lo and behold, I am taken away from the law firm website to the STEP website. On that website, I am presented with a 'find a STEP solicitor' button. I click it and end up instructing a totally different solicitor.

This is what happens nine times out of ten. If you display a qualification and link the logo to the qualification's website you will lose business. Let's go back to basics, the only purpose of your website is to make your telephone ring.

Qualifications are important, but you have to remember that they mean far more to you than they do to your clients, unless you take the time to explain to them why this makes you the best solicitor possible for their current needs. Therefore, instead of sending them away from your website, this is what you do:

- create a 'Why choose us/Our expertise' column on the right-hand side of your website, as outlined in the website design wireframe above;
- display any specialist qualification logos beneath it, with the name of the qualification;
- when they click on the logos, redirect them to a page on *your* website that explains what this qualification is and why your firm having it makes you a good fit for their needs; and

- end that page with your call to action, asking your prospect to make contact with you.

Suddenly you stop losing potential clients and instead justify why you should receive their instruction. Bingo!

PRESS COVERAGE: From celebrity news to reality television shows, people just cannot seem to get enough of the media in all formats. You can use this to your advantage. If you are featured in a regular local newspaper answering legal questions, let people know. Likewise, if you have ever commented on a topical legal matter on the basis of your expertise in that topic, again, let people know.

You will have seen on countless occasions on various websites comments such as 'As Seen On TV', 'Featured in *The Times*', or references to other media that the website owner has received some publicity from. This is done for a reason; it makes more people convinced that you must be the 'expert' that they are looking for.

You will notice on my website that I refer to being featured in the *Law Society Gazette*, the *Solicitors' Journal* and other publications. I do this for the same reason that I am advising you to do it. If I have been published by the *Gazette*, it helps to convince a solicitor visiting my website that I must know something about law firm marketing. You need to do the same.

This section should also feature in the 'proof of expertise' right-hand column of your website (as in the website design above).

Once again, use the logos from the press coverage that you are quoting to direct the visitor to another page on your website rather than to the media in question, because you don't want to send them away from your website, and include snippets of the coverage on that page.

As always, ensure you end that page with your call to action, asking the visitor to make contact with you to find out more about your legal services. You might also want to add on that page an additional call to action to any media representative reading the page, inviting them to contact you if they would like a quote from you on a legal topic.

NUMBER OF PEOPLE HELPED: This is one of my favourite methods for proving expertise, because it is at the heart of your service. If you have helped thousands of clients already, isn't that in itself a tick in the box for a potential client thinking about using your services?

Just imagine what they might think if they see on your website that you have already handled 'over 50,000' claims/conveyancing transactions/business start-ups?: 'Well, they must be doing something right to have helped that many people!'

I have used this information on all my business-to-consumer websites with great effect, including

- citing the number of enquiries handled on a claims company website;
- specifying the number of enquiries my website software Your Website Genie has handled for all my clients; and
- confirming on my law firm marketing website how many solicitors have already downloaded my free guide.

I believe this is one of the more powerful methods of proving expertise, so this information should normally be featured at or near the top of the website, so that it is one of the first things that people see on arrival. My only concern is that if every solicitor started to do it, it might lose some of its potency, but as I have been marketing law firms for many years now, I know that most solicitors, even if they think this is a good idea, will not actually implement it.

You also need to remember that most potential clients will look at no more than two or three law firm websites, so the chance of them finding two or three solicitors that have read this book *and* taken action is quite slight, unless of course they find your website, in which case you will clearly receive the instruction, and you and I will both be happy. Objectives achieved!

Content-Writing Essentials

When it comes to writing the content for each page, it is important to remember that most of your visitors will only be looking at one or two of them, so you need to cover certain core subjects on every page of your website.

Every page should follow the formula in the the following table to ensure a user can visit one page and obtain all of the information necessary to proceed to make an enquiry. Do not assume that your visitor will rummage around your website looking for everything. At most, you have two to three pages per visitor and less than two minutes, so every page must do everything possible to sell your services.

Website copywriting formula

Headline	Relate this to their likely state of mind as they arrive at this page. What will they be thinking or feeling? Will they be happy, worried or concerned? Whatever it is, start by talking about this, showing that you understand them from the start. Include the keywords you are targeting in the headline (the H1 tag) and whenever suitable in the body copy (without cramming it in when it makes no sense to the reader). For example, on the conveyancing page for a firm in Reading, the headline might be: **Conveyancing Solicitors, Reading** with the subheading: **Looking for the best solicitors in Reading to help you move quickly?**
Introductory paragraph	Continue to talk about the position that the client is in at that moment, expanding on the headline above. **If you are looking to move house, you may well be up against some fairly tight and important deadlines.**
Your solution	Reassure the visitor that you are the right business to help them deal with the challenge they are facing: **Moving house is one of the most stressful things you will do during your lifetime, so it is important that you have the very best legal advisor by your side to make the process as smooth as possible. Smithers Jones solicitors work for you and with you to meet your deadlines and to ensure that you move house how and when you want to.**

Your expertise	Expand on your expertise in this area and include bullet points explaining how you have already helped other people just like them. I do not talk about 'businesses', because you are selling your service to a person, whether you are selling business to business or business to individual legal services, so just sell to the person visiting your website at any given moment. **We help over 1,000 people move house every year and we use this experience to ensure that your move will proceed as quickly as possible and with the minimum of fuss.**
Review	Related to the service in question, and including a case study if available, describing the position of the client before they found you, what you did for them and how successfully it turned out. If possible, the review should answer some of the questions or concerns running through your visitor's mind as they as they read this page. **While I was initially a little concerned that I was paying more than some of the prices I had seen for my conveyance, I am absolutely delighted that I did. Smithers Jones went well beyond my expectations and made the process so much more straightforward than I was expecting. If you are thinking of asking them to help you move home, I would strongly advise you to go ahead. You will not regret it.**
Costs	You have to deal with the elephant in the room, but if your initial contact with new clients is free, that is all you need to stress at this point. Remember that your only task from this page is to sell the first contact with you. Ideally, the testimonial before this section should specify that this first contact is free, but if it does not, what you are looking to do at this point is to take away any concerns and encourage your prospect to call you. **All initial enquiries are completely free of charge, so please do not hesitate to call us. We will provide you with a fixed price quotation/ a choice of funding methods and we can even offer payment by instalments if required, so please do get in touch today.**
Call to action	You must offer options for how your visitor can contact you as this will increase the volume of enquiries that you receive. I learned this the hard way by initially offering only telephone enquiries, but then seeing enquiries rise dramatically when I added an enquiry form (see below). Here is an example of a good call to action: **Make a Free Enquiry** Call us now on 01234 56789, email **info@smithersjones.co.uk** or complete our **Free Online Enquiry** [*links to your enquiry form page*] for a free, no-obligation discussion and let us explain your legal rights and options.

Dual Readership Path	People read websites in different ways. Some people will read every single word, others will simply skim down the page to check it covers all that they want it to. If you do not ensure that your content appeals to both types of reader, you will miss opportunities to win instructions. The following items will ensure that you appeal to as many of your website visitors as possible.
	IMAGES: It is important to include an image for the skim readers, as it is part of your dual readership path to ensure both detail readers and skim readers are kept happy.
	This image should include 'alt tag' and 'title tag' to target the keywords on the page – good for AdWords and search marketing (see earlier sections).
	In most cases, the image should be thumbnail sized. You are not looking for the image to take over from the content, just to enhance or supplement it. A small image will therefore do the job nicely.
	BULLET POINTS: Break up the content with bullet points – again for your dual readership path, – in line with the following example:
	• 400+ words per page.
	• Be approachable and friendly. Don't use legal jargon.
	• Ensure enough pages for each type of service to convince your prospects of your expertise.
	• Ensure all the content focuses on the benefits for clients – remember, Clients First.
	SUBHEADINGS: One long page of content with no subheadings is very difficult to read. Ensure that you place a heading above each section of content on each page to break it up. This, alongside images and bullet points, will dramatically increase the readability of your page and therefore the enquiries that you receive from it.

Defending solicitors with a well promoted website

My area of practice is regulatory and professional discipline law, specialising in particular in the solicitors' profession.

I have for more than 20 years prosecuted on behalf of the SRA and its predecessors, and defended solicitors appearing before the SDT.

I have presented more than 650 cases before the SDT over the years.

I now exclusively defend solicitors who are the subject of investigation by the SRA and/or who are facing a hearing before the SDT.

I previously had a website which was, to an extent, invisible.

Given the move towards pure defence work, it was important that my profile be reignited so the solicitors' profession were aware I was available to assist them.

I reviewed and amended my current website to one designed solely with the intention of creating new enquiries for my services. I added more details about my services and many more pages explaining exactly what I do to ensure that I proved my expertise and answered all my prospects' potential questions. Every page has a strong but simple call to action encouraging the visitor to contact me.

Once my new website went live I immediately started using Google AdWords which has produced a steady line of new enquiries from potential clients and continues to do so on an ongoing basis.

JONATHAN GOODWIN, SOLICITOR ADVOCATE.

Page-Appropriate Content

Your Home Page

The home page is a slight exception to the rules for content. Whereas the objective for most pages is to encourage your visitor to make contact with you, your home page's objective is to get the visitor to the page that they are looking for as quickly as possible.

This is because most people arriving at your home page already know you or you have been recommended to you. They have typed in your firm's name and landed on your home page, so you need to get them to the place that they are looking for. This means that after a very brief introduction, to confirm that they are indeed in the right place, you need to provide easy options for them to click through to:

- Your main service pages
- Your contact page
- Your enquiry form
- Your reviews (testimonials)

Include a call to action at the bottom of the page and you have all you need for your home page.

Some people seem to fixate on their home page, but it really only needs to take care of the points above. For this reason, it does not necessarily need to follow the three-column layout that I recommended in the website wireframe earlier, although you will notice that my own home page still does this. It works well for me.

Navigation

MAKE IT ALPHABETICAL: The navigation for your legal services should be alphabetical. It is the only logical way for your clients to find what they are looking for.

What usually happens is that websites list services in the order of their importance to the law firm owner of the website. All this does is tell your competitors where you make most of your money. Do you really want to do that?

INCLUDE THE FREE ENQUIRY FORM LINK: when you accept that you must have an enquiry form, the next thing you have to do is to ensure that it is included in your navigation, so that people can jump straight to it if they reach the point of being ready to make an enquiry, but you haven't made it easy for them to do so on the page that they find themselves on.

EXPANDING NAVIGATION: when someone lands inside a legal service section on your website they should instantly be able to see a list of all the pages within that section, so that they know you are experts (two-minute trust builder system).

It is easy to set this up – your website designer can do this for you. The point is to make it easy for your prospects to find all the pages within a section, so that if they land on the wrong one, they can quickly find the right one.

WILLS AND PROBATE: these are two completely different services. They might be handled by the same person in your firm, but they are not the same service. As a potential client, if I am looking to make a Will, I expect to find an item on your navigation called 'Wills'. Likewise, if I am looking for a probate solicitor, I expect to find an item on your navigation called 'Probate'. That is only logical, isn't it? So please do not make the mistake that most of your competitors make by lumping them into one item on the navigation. You don't necessarily have to make two completely different sections in your website (although, bearing in mind what I said earlier about the two-minute trust builder system above, I would), but at least have them as two separate items in your navigation.

Your Enquiry Form Page

This is one of the most important pages on your website. Let me assure you, based on my testing of real legal websites, if you do not have an enquiry form you will miss out on many enquiries for your services.

The form itself should be as short as possible and offer simple introductory content, such as the following:

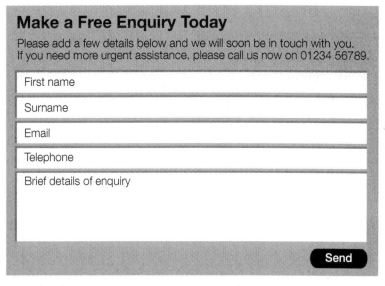

What happens next is important, in that on completion of the enquiry form your visitor *must* be redirected to a new page, for example,' smithersjones.com/thank-you'. The purpose of this is that it will allow you to place a piece of tracking code on this page that will show you how many enquiries have been generated each month, and, more importantly, what people typed into the search engine or which of your Google AdWords keywords turned into a new enquiry. So many firms fail to do this and simply have a tiny pop-up message appear on the page, which is both hard for the user to spot but more importantly prevents you from tracking what is working to make your telephone ring.

The second key point is that if you are smart and follow my advice to have a call centre handle all the telephone enquiries from your marketing initiatives, especially your website, the call centre should have a separate enquiry form that it completes each time it handles an enquiry for you, and this should be redirected to a separate thank-you page on your website, such as 'smithersjones .co.uk/thank-you-call-centre'. This has several purposes:

- it will allow you to see how many enquiries they are handling for you, so that you can see the value they are bringing to you;
- once an enquiry is submitted, it will be sent to your firm instantly, so that the details will be in front of the person the call is transferred to, saving them the time and trouble of repeating the information already provided (and making you look far more professional than the other firms that the potential client has already spoken with who did not do this); and
- You can add some additional questions to this form, which your call centre will gladly complete for you. These should be:
  – How did you find us today?
  – If they say 'search', the follow-on question should be 'As you are in front of your screen, can you let me know what you typed into the search engine to find, please?' This question will be answered more often than not (I know from experience).
  – If they say 'recommended', the call centre can ask the name of the person and/or business that introduced them to you, so you can add this to your referral tracking sheet (see Chapter 12).

– If they say 'advertisement' the call centre should ask for the name and date of the publication.

I think you have probably got the gist of this now. You need to know how every enquiry finds your law firm, so that you know exactly which methods of marketing are producing results for you. I know from experience that if you ask your receptionist or fee earners to ask these questions they will find an excuse not to do so and will usually just put down 'existing client/recommendation' as it is usually the easiest option to select. However, you need to know the real answer. A call centre will obtain this for you.

It is so much better to run your law firm knowing exactly what it is that you do that makes your telephone ring, as then you can do more of that and spend less on the methods that are simply not working for you.

Your Blog

Once you have a website, it is vital that you don't simply forget about it. Let me explain why with a case study.

New content

Several of my clients over the years have followed my advice and consistently added new content to their websites every month. What has happened in each case? Even with the numerous Google algorithm changes that have taken place over the last few years (the method that Google uses to assess which websites should appear closest to the top of their search results), the same thing happens to these websites: they regularly attract thousands of visitors, and these visitors make enquiries about their services.

My advice is that you add at least two articles a month (by outsourcing to a copywriter, of course), or as many as two a week. As with all marketing, consistency is crucial to build your momentum. If you do this for two or three months and then stop, you will not see many results. If you do it every month you will see a steady increase in both volume of visitors to your website and number of enquiries received from your website about your services.

I sometimes have to laugh, though … In my 'more clients now' calls with solicitors, one of the questions I always ask is how many people visit their website every month. The most common response is that they do not know, followed by the comment 'Not a great many, but one of our blog posts seems to do really well and attract a few hundred visitors every month.'

'Excellent news', I say, then I add, 'So, knowing that blogging works so well, how frequently do you add new blog posts then?' 'Erm, never,' is always the response.

If you have written one blog post that attracts regular visitors to your website, what would happen if you had 10 or 20 of these blog posts? You know the answer, of course. You would obtain ten to twenty times the volume of visitors and a corresponding increase in the volume of enquiries that you receive about your services.

Once you have a website, please ensure that one of the things you do consistently is to add new content to it. When you do that, you will soon start to see some results.

In the next section I will detail the metrics that you need to check once a month (which will only take a few minutes of your time), to show you how well you are doing so that you keep on doing it – or keep on keeping on, as I like to say.

Responsive Websites

It is vital that you have a 'responsive' website, because Google says so. If you do not, Google will not send people who are browsing on smaller devices such as mobile phones or iPads to your website. As this is now accounts for as much as 50% of visitors to law firm websites, you are instantly missing 50% of your potential audience if you do not have a mobile-responsive website.

How do you know if your website is mobile responsive or not? Simple, open your website on your desktop browser, then press the minimise page box in the top right-hand corner of your browser.

Checking Your Website's Mobile Responsiveness

Now, go to the bottom right of the browser and, using the resize arrows, make the browser continually smaller, until you have reduced it to mobile size. Throughout this process, if your website is mobile responsive, it will constantly be resizing to fit the browser size available. If it doesn't do this, but just shows the website getting smaller and smaller, you do not have a mobile responsive website, so you will need to change that.

There is a video walk-through of this test in the resources section if you would like to see it in action: www.samsonconsulting .co.uk/growth

Clever Website Urls/addresses

Your website address should be your firm's name or as close to it as possible. While there used to be some mileage in using a clever website address which explained to Google which service you provided, for example, www.personalinjurysolicitors.co.uk, Google changed the rules and this will actually have a negative impact on your website performance now, so don't do it.

One Website or Many?

Once again, there was a time when having a main website plus one, two or ten niche websites for each of your legal services might have been useful. That time has gone. I see so many firms running around chasing this idea while their main law firm website is still woefully inadequate and doesn't deploy any of my proven tactics.

If you still think this is a good idea (it really isn't) let me urge you to ensure that your main website is staggeringly good, follows every piece of advice above, and has at least 1,000 pages and over 1,000 reviews before you move on to creating another website of any kind to promote your legal services.

However, I promise you that if you follow the advice in the preceding paragraphs, you will have too much work coming in to even think about creating another website.

Your Website Designer/Developer/Marketing Agency

I have stayed away from caffeine for an hour before writing this section. I have meditated, thought of lovely holiday destinations and put on some very mellow music, yet still as I start typing I can feel my hackles starting to rise and my blood warming up.

I have seen countless website designers ruin law firm websites. It is not necessarily that they are malicious, although some are, it is just that they think they know best, yet none of them do, or none that I have met yet do, and I have met many.

Let me explain what I mean, because this is important for your law firm success. After reading this section of this book, you might decide that I have made some good points and you need to make some changes to your website. You compile a list of these changes and present them to your website designer. Let's consider a few of the things that you might ask him to do and I'll tell you what his responses will be, based on the thousands of times that I have been through this irksome process.

YOU I would like my website below the main header to follow a three-column layout, with navigation on the left, content in the middle and then a right-hand column with an enquiry form, testimonials and some other important features.

WEBSITE DESIGNER No, what I think you should do is just have navigation at the top, then have an infinity-scrolling website that goes on and on forever, but is really beautiful to look at.

YOU Look, I am being advised by a law firm marketing specialist who has tested various design layouts and this method works best, so that is what I want to do.

WEBSITE SLAYER Well, I don't agree with him. I have no proof that my methods work, but I like to design something different every time I sit down to create a website, and all that matters to me is my design integrity. If I do what you are asking me it won't look unique and I won't want to put it on my portfolio page to show how brilliant I am.

YOU Fine, I will go somewhere else then.

WEBSITE SLAUGHTERER Oh no, don't do that. I need the work. I will do whatever you want me to do now that you have made it clear that you are serious.

Your website designer will do as you tell them when you make it clear that you know what you want, but the second that they spot any weakness I promise you that they will try to create a website that interests them rather than one that will make your telephone ring.

I have met hundreds of solicitors who have websites that their designer was instrumental in creating, often for several thousands of pounds, yet they never produce any new clients. If you follow my advice you will create a website that consistently delivers new clients to you. Once your website is live, if you consistently add new content to it and use Google AdWords (see next chapter), the numbers will rise even more.

However, if you allow your website designer to bully you into accepting the website that he or she wants to create, as so often happens, you will not generate clients from your website, which will make your practice far less profitable than it could or should be. If you end up struggling to meet your mortgage payments, your website designer won't be there to help you. They will have moved on to slaughtering the next victim's business with a 'beautifully designed' website that will not make the telephone ring for them either.

I bet you are glad I used all of those relaxation methods before I wrote this chapter, aren't you? I just get so frustrated for all of the messes that I have had to clear up over the years. All I want to do is to make your life easier and help you to attract clients more consistently, so when someone gets in the way of my objectives I don't take it sitting down. You shouldn't either. Be strong. Ensure your designer follows your instructions and then sit back and enjoy the results.

Content Management System

In the world of the web, CMS stands for content management system, in other words, the software that allows you to make changes to the words and images on your website.

There are many different types of content management system

available for law firm websites, but please bear in mind that if someone offers you their 'bespoke content management system', what this ultimately means is that you will be tied to that system and their service for as long as you want to keep that website. Therefore, when you do leave, you will have to start building your new website from scratch.

Now, a bespoke system may still be a good choice for you based on a number of factors. For example, I work with a company which provides an excellent law firm website design service, in that they charge a very low up-front cost, but then a small monthly fee. This makes it a very accessible service to any size of law firm. However, it does tie you to their content management system.

The alternative is to use an off-the-shelf content management system, the most popular by far being WordPress. This system has been developed from a simple piece of blogging software to one that runs millions of websites worldwide. It is free and there are thousands of website designers who know how to make changes to it. This has the real benefit that if you ever fall out with your current website designer (see above), you can easily find another one to take over control instantly, with very little trouble. It also means that when you do decide that you want a complete website redesign, it is a very much more straightforward process.

What you must never do, as a solicitor, is to obtain a 'free' website which proudly displays at the bottom of the page 'Another free website from . . .' Why? You are a professional service provider. What does having a free website say about you to your clients? Does it make you look like the best available solicitor for their legal needs or like one who cuts corners? I believe there is only one correct answer to that point, so I shall move on. Don't do it.

The Best Website Design Process

If you are considering setting up a new website now or in the future, I want to ensure that you follow the system that will give you the best and timeliest results. Here it is:

1. Leave your old website live until your new one is ready to replace it. A bad, older website is infinitely better than none at all, or, worse still a 'website under construction' notice.

2. Instruct your new website designer by providing very clear instructions on exactly what it is that you need, including a list of all the pages on your current website. This will ensure that you can receive a fixed price quotation for your services. Prices usually escalate when you keep adding pages and sections. Mapping out the entire website before design starts will allow you to avoid this problem.

3. Agree the new design and ask your designer to copy all your old content across to the new website, then go live.

4. Add or change the content when the website is live. It is the creation or editing of the content that *always* delays any website design project, so my strong advice is to wait until the new website is live before tackling this. As your new website is likely to be built with a content management system, it will be easy for you, or preferably your designer, to add the content when the new website is live. If you decide your old website is simply not good enough, perhaps because it doesn't follow my suggested design layout and doesn't include an enquiry form, getting the new design up and running as fast as possible is the most important thing.

If you need any help, please feel free to ask away. Download the resources from www.samsonconsulting.co.uk/growth and you will receive all my contact details.

Get Useful Information from Your Website

Google Analytics

Once you have a decent website, it is vital that you track its performance, so that you can see the results of your hard work and measure your rewards.

You must have Google Analytics on your website because it will show you not only how many people are finding your website, how much time they spend on it and how many pages they viewed, but also some other really useful information.

For example, if you set it up correctly you will be able to see the search terms that people typed into Google to find your website. This is really useful, because it

- shows that you are getting some results from your regular efforts to grow your website;
- provides you with more ideas for blogs, articles and legal service pages; and
- allows you to spend some time on your most visited pages, to get them working harder to make your telephone ring.

You must insist that your website developer adds Google Analytics for you. Google provides lots of useful videos on how you can do this, but they may be out of date before this book is published, so I will just give you the most important points about Google Analytics.

The landing page you see when you log in to Google Analytics defaults to the last 7 days and the most important metrics are the ones below.

SESSIONS: These are the total number of visits to your website. Google will give a more convoluted definition, but this, in short, is what a session is.

USERS: These are the unique visitors to your website (so this number will be lower than the one for sessions because some people will visit more than once).

PAGE VIEWS: The total number of pages viewed during the time period. Anything around twice the number of sessions shows that your website is working quite well, in that people aren't just landing on your site then jumping straight off it.

PAGES PER SESSION: Same as above, really; you are looking for around two page views per session or more.

AVG. SESSION DURATION: The average session duration, which, as I say, used to be around two minutes (hence the two-minute trust builder) but now is down to around 90 seconds.

Google gives you plentiful information, but here are a couple of points that can add some real punch to your marketing.

Search Queries Used to Find Your Website

To access this information, you log in to Google Analytics, then, as highlighted in the image below, select 'Acquisition', then 'Search console' and then 'Queries'. You might at first be asked to link to your search console (ask your website developer to set this up for you, or Google to see how you can do it), then you will be presented with the search queries that have led to your website being listed in the Google search results.

Please note, Google defaults to only showing you the first 10 results, so make sure you change that setting to 1,000 or more, so you can have a proper look through your results.

Most successful search queries

	Search Query	Clicks	Impressions	CTR	Average Position
		306 % of Total: 100.00% (306)	13,231 % of Total: 100.00% (13,231)	2.31% Avg for View: 2.31% (0.00%)	45 Avg for View: 45 (0.00%)
	1. (not set)	230 (75.16%)	3,786 (28.61%)	6.08%	27
	2. Samson Consulting	10 (3.27%)	18 (0.14%)	55.56%	1.7
Acquisition	3. Nick Jervis	9 (2.94%)	29 (0.22%)	31.03%	1.0
Overview	4. Legal newsletter names	7 (2.29%)	21 (0.16%)	33.33%	1.0
>> All Traffic	5. Bluestone or Centerparcs	5 (1.63%)	61 (0.46%)	8.20%	7.0
>> Adwords	6. Marketing ideas for solicitors	5 (1.63%)	44 (0.33%)	11.36%	1.2
Search Consol NEW	7. Personal injury leads	4 (1.31%)	198 (1.50%)	2.02%	8.4
Landing Pages	8. Articles of association template	3 (0.98%)	87 (0.66%)	3.45%	11
Countries	9. Buying a solicitors practice	3 (0.98%)	17 (0.13%)	17.65%	4.7
Devices	10. Personal injury lead generation	3 (0.98%)	78 (0.59%)	3.85%	3.0
Queries	11. Setting up a law firm in England	2 (0.65%)	22 (0.17%)	9.09%	8.0

SEARCH QUERY: The phrase typed into Google that led to your website being displayed in the search results.

CLICKS: The total number of people clicking through from the search query onto your website.

IMPRESSIONS: The number of times that your website appeared in the search results for the search term in question. What is important to note here is that this shows you how many times the particular search term was entered into Google causing your website to be listed. Obviously the higher the number of impressions the better, but how many clicks you receive will depend on the position you find yourself in in the search results (see below).

CTR – CLICK-THROUGH RATE: This is the clicks divided by the number of impressions.

AVERAGE POSITION: How close to the top spot your website appeared in the search results.

Improve Your Website Pages to Generate More Visitors

What I am looking for from these figures is a search term with a lot of impressions, but one for which my website might not be particularly close to the top of the results. I know then that it is worth spending some time making this page even more attractive to Google.

For example, one of the search results shows that the term 'personal injury leads' had 198 searches over the course of the last 30 days, but that my website only had 4 clicks as it was in average position 8.4.

Now, if I wanted to get more of those 198 people to click onto my website this is what I would do:

1. type that search term into Google and see which page on my website is appearing in or around 8 places down in the search results (it won't always be in the exact average position of course, but usually within a range of +/-5);

2. go to that website page and improve it (thereby giving Google more reasons to list it higher in the search results) by doing the following:

    – adding more content to the page, especially content including the keywords in question – 'personal injury leads' – so that the page becomes more authoritative on this search term. In looking at the page in question I can see that it is quite short. It only has around 300 words, so I know that adding another 300–400 words could make a substantial difference;

- ensuring that the search term appears in the 'title' tag, 'description' tag and 'H1' tag (see earlier); and
- adding an image with 'alt' and 'title' tags containing the keywords 'personal injury leads'. If you do not have an image on your pages, adding one gives you another chance to tell Google what the page is all about, so it is well worth doing.

Here is the code I would add behind the image.

<img class='alignright size-full wp-image-264' src='http://www.samsonconsulting.co.uk/wp-content/uploads/2015/07/lawboard-personal-injury-small.jpg' alt='Personal Injury Leads' title='Personal Injury Leads' width='125' height='219' />

Remember, you have to include both of these tags, even though they say exactly the same thing, because some internet browsers read the 'alt' tag, others the 'title' tag. If you only use one, you miss opportunities to attract more visitors.

Using Google Analytics to Find New Content Ideas

In addition to using Google Analytics to see what people are typing into Google so that you can improve the content on these pages, you can also use this information to generate more ideas for content for your website.

In my example above, the search term and the page that visitors are referred to are closely linked, but often this is not the case. Let me show you an example.

Link between search term and page

Search Query	Clicks	Impressions	CTR	Average Position
428. how to market legal services	0 (0.00%)	29 (0.19%)	0.00%	35

The term, 'how to market legal services' is searched for 29 times a month (as shown in the impressions column). You can see that I am position 35 on average, which is why I attract no clicks. No one is going past the first page, so I have two options: I can improve the page content as suggested above, or I can write a new article directly addressing this search term.

When I take a look at my listing in or around position 35, I see that I am on 'Page 4 of about 101,000,000 results'.

Page 4 of about 101,000,000 results (0.42 seconds)

Legal Marketing Services | Marketing For Solicitors
https://www.samsonconsulting.co.uk ▼
Marketing For Solicitors Specialist! Need Legal **Marketing** Services Help To Win You New Clients? Samson Consulting - **Marketing** For Solicitors Made Easy.

This is my home page. I would not rewrite my home page to address this search term as that is not the purpose of my home page, so the best option is to write a new article that does so.

If you did this exercise just once a month, finding good search terms with a reasonable number of searches each month that are currently being directed to the wrong page on your website, and writing an article that addresses the specific search term, you would have 12 very 'prospect-focused' new pages by the end of the year. If just two of these pages make it to the top, or close to the top, of Google's listing (which is much more likely to happen now that they are addressing a specific issue), you will generate hundreds more visits to your website every month. Some of these visitors will become clients, so it's an exercise well worth undertaking.

Other Website Software

There are many useful software tools for websites that can save you time and generate more clients. However, software being software, they are constantly changing and evolving. What might be brilliant today may be out of date in a few months, so although I have covered Google Analytics in some detail here, I will let you have my latest software recommendations when you access the free resources section here: www.samsonconsulting.co.uk/growth

The type of software that I like to use includes tools that automatically generate more enquiries from your website, from automated live chat, outsourced 24/7 live chat (where someone answers questions on your behalf all day, every day) to tools that check that you have set up the all-important 'behind the scenes' title tags and meta tags.

Monitoring Your Website's Key Performance Indicators (KPIs)

Monitoring your website KPIs is an incredibly powerful motivational tool. Why? Well, you might at some stage lose a bit of interest or head of steam. However, when you measure your website performance each month and see the number of visitors increasing, the number of enquiries increasing, and, most importantly, the number of instructions from all this increasing, it keeps you going when otherwise you might think of stopping. This is something that you absolutely must do.

Here is an example of the KPI's that you should be monitoring each month.

Monthly monitoring of KPIs

Row	Detail	Month 1	Month 2	Month 3	Month 4
1	Total visitors (sessions)	1,299			
2	Page views	2,620			
3	Pages per session	2.02			
4	Avg. session duration	1.48			
5	Enquiries	30			
6	Instructions from enquiries	15			
7	Conversion percentage	50%			
8	New articles added	4			
9	New testimonials added	2			
10	New case studies added	1			

The first four rows can be obtained from your Google Analytics account, as shown below.

KPI Data from Google Analytics

Sessions	Users	Page Views	Pages/Session	Avg. Session Duration
1,299	1,038	2,620	2.02	00:01:48

This is where you can see the power of the two-minute trust builder, in that the average duration of the sessions is just under two minutes, and the average number of pages viewed is 2.02. This is for my own website, so I beat the average time of 90 seconds because solicitors tend to be 'detail' people by their nature, wanting to read a bit more information before taking action. Your clients are a mixture of detail and scan readers, so 90 seconds or more is what you should expect – or hope – to see. If you are seeing anything less than that, then you need to work through the content of this chapter to improve your website.

I have included rows 8 to 10 because, as I always say, 'what gets measured gets better'. If you add more content to your website each month in the form of articles or blogs, over time you will see the number of visitors to your website increase.

If, in addition to this, you add more case studies and testimonials too, you will also see a rise in the number of potential clients making contact with you, as you will be developing an important element of the two-minute trust builder.

Once you have your basic website details, you need to add in the other figures. There is a spreadsheet for monitoring the leads generated available when you sign up for the resources at www .samsonconsulting.co.uk/growth. You can use this to complete rows 4 and 5 (leads and instructions). Row 7 is a really useful calculation to carry out using the answers from rows 5 and 6.

What conversion figures should you expect? The answer to this question depends on a number of factors, such as how niche your service is (expect higher conversion figures) or how complex your legal matters are (for example, medical negligence will convert at a much lower rate than conveyancing).

However, you should be aiming for between 20% and 60% conversion from enquiries received. The only thing that matters is that you track your rate and work your socks off to improve it once you know what it is, using the information in the chapter on client conversion earlier in the book to do this. It is some of the best investment of your time in marketing your law firm, and a key part of the law firm growth formula.

A starting point you should be aiming for, across the board, is at least 30%. Many firms that I start working with are operating at or below 10%, so I start improving their conversion processes first, knowing that this will provide them with the biggest return on investment of their time.

—

Your website is a vital tool. It is open 24 hours a day, 7 days a week. It is the first place someone visits when you are recommended to them. If it is not up to the task of generating enquiries, it will cost you more instructions than you could ever imagine. However, if you make it the best law firm website that it can be, it will continue to reward you with more clients, month after month.

Chapter 11

Artery 3: Google AdWords

Think back to the peacocks versus elephants marketing example earlier on in the book – you haven't forgotten it, have you? No? Good, I didn't think so. You want to use the marketing that brings people to you at the precise moment that they are looking for a solicitor. Google AdWords is one of these methods.

Let's say Jim is buying his first house. He has put in an offer that has been accepted, so he now needs to find a solicitor. He asks his friends if they can recommend anyone, but of course if they have used a solicitor at any time in the past few years they won't have heard from them since the transaction concluded, because their solicitors haven't read this book, so he does what everyone else does and heads online.

He opens Google, types in the name of his town plus the service he is looking for and is presented with these results:

Google Search Results

Below is a list of 'fake' results that I have created to show you how AdWords works. *I was advised by my publisher not to use live results for copyright reasons.*

About 177,000 results (0.60 seconds)

Manchester Conveyancers – Fixed Fee & No Hidden Extras
Ad www.manchesterconveyancers.co.uk ▼
Fixed Fee Property **Conveyancers** Manchester. Call Today

£250 Fixed Price Service – Special Offer This Month Only
Ad www.fixedpriceconveyancing.com ▼
Specialist, Quick **Conveyancers**. £250 This Month Only
Services: Sale, Purchase, Remortgage Leases
Quote For Sale- Quote For Purchase – Remortgage Quote – Happy Clients

Conveyancing Solicitors Near You – All Conveyancing Services
Ad www.conveyancingnearyou.co.uk ▼
Nationwide **Conveyancing** Service. Free Online **Conveyancing** Quote.
Pay Nothing If No Move ~ ISO 9001 ~ UK Wide Service ~ Free Instant Quote
Free Quote ~ Online Reviews ~ Our Service For You ~ Contact Us

Specialist Conveyancing Solicitors – Over 95% Client Satisfaction
Ad www.specialistconveyancing.co.uk ▼
Specialists in property sales and purchasing. Call us for a free consultation.
Services: Sales, Purchases, Remortgages, Leasehold
Range Of Services ~ Liverpool Offices ~ Press Coverage

UK Conveyancing Lawyers – ABC & Co Law
www.abc-law.co.uk ▼
ABC Law specialise in property services and have served Manchester since
1985. We will take care of you.

Results 1 to 4 are all Google AdWords results. They are the first four results that the searcher sees. It is not until result number 5 that you see a firm that is not paying (directly) to be in the results. You will also notice that 2, 3 and 4 are all occupying significantly more space than number 1. This is because they are making the most of the Google AdWords features which I will explore in this chapter

I will cover this situation in more detail later in this chapter, but for now I just wanted to make the point that Google AdWords works well because it is peacock/attraction marketing in its purest form. Someone looking for your service sees your advertisement, clicks on it and lands on your website. If you have followed the advice in the previous chapter, ensuring that your website is very well presented and drafted, you will get the telephone call, or the online enquiry that allows you to call the prospect. If you have the meaningful conversation when you speak with your prospect you will secure the instruction more often than not, even if you charge more than some of your competitors.

If you have tried Google AdWords before and it did not work for you, more often than not it is because you were not doing it properly. I am sorry to be blunt, but 98% of the time it works for solicitors, so unless you really are in that 2% category, it will have failed for one of these reasons:

- you didn't spend enough;
- you didn't make full use of all of the available features;
- you sent people to pages on your website that could simply never turn a visitor into a new prospect.

All of these things, individually, can stop a campaign being successful. Together they can totally derail a Google AdWords campaign at the same time as taking a fair chunk of your hard-earned money.

I have some great news for those of you who have not yet tried Google AdWords because you believe:

- I never click on those advertisements so no one else will either; or
- No one buys legal services from a Google search.

You are completely wrong!

If, up till now, you have been thinking either or both of these things, by telling you that you are wrong I have just opened a significant opportunity for you to win a substantial volume of new client instructions that you are currently missing.

Google makes around $20 billion per quarter solely from Google AdWords. In my small sector of the legal world, my clients spend in excess of one million pounds a year on Google AdWords. Let me assure you that they only do this because they know that AdWords puts a significant amount more money in terms of billed profits into their law firms than it takes out of them. Those figures should prove to you beyond reasonable doubt that Google AdWords works for solicitors.

Now let me show you what you need to do to make Google AdWords work properly.

Manage Your AdWords Manager

Let me start by reminding you what my objective is with this book. I want to provide you with the knowledge you need to manage the suppliers who are running your marketing campaigns for you. I don't want you to do your own marketing, especially when it comes to Google AdWords, because it will be a complete and utter waste of your valuable time, and, to put it bluntly, it is very unlikely you will do it as well as an outsourced supplier.

I have been running Google AdWords campaigns for my own business and for clients since 2004. AdWords changes and evolves constantly. Unless you are working with it every day, it is hard to reach the levels of expertise that you need to reach to make it successful for you.

If you do want to scale the heights of becoming a successful Google AdWords campaign manager, you will fail in so many other areas of running your law firm that it will be a bitter-tasting success. If you are genuinely serious about growing your law firm, you must be in control of the numbers and manage your outsourced suppliers, but you shouldn't do it all yourself. It is simply impossible for you to do that. Therefore, my aim with this chapter is to set out vital statistics of an AdWords campaign and other information you will need, so that you can manage your supplier to do it for you.

The Basics

I mentioned that Google AdWords is more of a science, so how does this science work? Well, the great news is that it isn't just about paying Google the most money to get to the number one position in the search results. That being said, if you do Google AdWords badly, Google will have no problem taking your money from you even though you might not be getting any results.

The basic formula that Google uses to decide who sits in position number one is called 'ad rank', and in simple terms, it works like this:

Quality score × amount of your bid = ad rank

I will examine the details of your quality score in a moment, but first, let me show you why it isn't just about bidding the largest amount to get to number one, although, as you can see from the formula, that is a factor.

Examples of ad rank calculations

Advertiser	Amount of bid	Quality score	Ad rank	Position In Google Results
1	£5.00	2	10	4
2	£3.00	5	15	1
3	£2.00	6	12	3
4	£1.50	9	13.5	2

Your keywords, plus your advertisements, plus your landing pages create your quality score, which, when combined with your bid, leads to your ad rank. This score determines which position your advertisement will appear in for the relevant search terms. The higher the ad rank score, the higher you will be listed in the paid search results.

In this example, Advertiser 2 will be in position 1 even though they are bidding £2 less per click than Advertiser 1. The more interesting part is that Advertiser 4 will be in position 2 even though they are bidding the lowest amount for each click.

This is the beauty of the science of Google AdWords. This is why I know that law firms with smaller marketing budgets can, and frequently do, beat large law firms with vast marketing budgets. Many of my clients consistently appear above competitors that operate on a national scale with marketing budgets many times higher than those of my clients. I love it! They achieve this by having a better-quality score for their keywords, which then allows them to bid less than the big guns but still achieve a better ad rank.

So, how do you improve your quality score? There are three key factors that determine your quality score:

- the content of your advertisement;
- your keywords (the words that you feature to attract people to your website); and
- the page on your website that your visitor is redirected to (your landing page).

The ideal scenario is that your visitor types in their search term, they see your advertisement at the top of Google AdWords and it matches what they are looking for, so they click your advertisement and are redirected to a page on your website that addresses the topic that they have typed into Google, which encourages them to make contact with you. Bingo! You have a good new prospect.

It sounds simple, doesn't it? The truth of the matter is, in its purest form, it really is that simple. However, it does take some time, lots of tweaking and constant measuring to achieve this objective. It might help if I show you examples of good and bad advertisements.

Imagine Jane types into Google 'business solicitor Bristol' and is presented with this advertisement.

A poor match

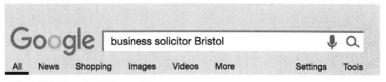

About 177,000 results (0.60 seconds)

Compensation Specialists – Start Your Claim Today

`Ad` www.compensationclaimspecialists.com/claimnow▼

No Win No Fee – Specialist Solicitors – Free Claim Enquiry
UK Wide Service ~ Thousands Helped Already ~ No Obligation
Services: Car Accidents, Criminal Injuries, Factory Accidents, Work Accidents
Calculator Your Value– Schedule A Call – Claim Today – Why Choose Us

This is based on a real search that I carried out when I typed in Jane's search term above. The contents have been changed to ensure the business remains anonymous, but I wanted to show you what can happen if Google AdWords is not handled correctly.

Can you see the problems with the advertisement versus what I typed into Google? I was looking for a business solicitor in Bristol, instead I am presented with an advertisement for a compensation claim expert. The advertisement heading does not match what I typed into Google, nor does the content or any other parts of the advertisement. The quality score is likely to be very low, meaning that the advertiser must have been prepared to pay a lot of money for each click for this advertisement even to be displayed.

The chances of Jane clicking on the advertisement are low, because the advertisement copy does not match her search term, and even if she does click on to it, the page she is redirected to is not going to match her needs either.

For the good example, let us use Jim's search for a conveyancing, as we did above, which produced the following results.

A good match

About 177,000 results (0.60 seconds)

Manchester Conveyancers – Fixed Fee & No Hidden Extras
Ad www.manchesterconveyancers.co.uk ▼
Fixed Fee Property **Conveyancers** Manchester. Call Today

£250 Fixed Price Service – Special Offer This Month Only
Ad www.fixedpriceconveyancing.com ▼
Specialist, Quick **Conveyancers**. £250 This Month Only
Services: Sale, Purchase, Remortgage Leases
Quote For Sale- Quote For Purchase – Remortgage Quote – Happy Clients

Conveyancing Solicitors Near You – All Conveyancing Services
Ad www.conveyancingnearyou.co.uk ▼
Nationwide **Conveyancing** Service. Free Online **Conveyancing** Quote.
Pay Nothing If No Move ~ ISO 9001 ~ UK Wide Service ~ Free Instant Quote
Free Quote ~ Online Reviews ~ Our Service For You ~ Contact Us

Specialist Conveyancing Solicitors – Over 95% Client Satisfaction
Ad www.specialistconveyancing.co.uk ▼
Specialists in property sales and purchasing. Call us for a free consultation.
Services: Sales, Purchases, Remortgages, Leasehold
Range Of Services ~ Liverpool Offices ~ Press Coverage

UK Conveyancing Lawyers – ABC & Co Law
www.abc-law.co.uk ▼
ABC Law specialise in property services and have served Manchester since
1985. We will take care of you.

Advertiser number 1 is the only one that mentions Manchester in the title. Sadly, however, Advertiser one does not make full use of all of the AdWords facilities, so the advertisement is only three lines deep when it could be six lines deep, as in the fourth advertisement, yet this is one targets a completely different geographical location, Liverpool.

Therefore, despite advertiser number one not making use of all of the AdWords features (which I will go through in detail below), Jim is still most likely to click on it because it mentions

'Manchester', which is clearly important to him. The advertisement can definitely be improved on, though, so let us look at what goes into making a really good Google AdWords advertisement that achieves a high Ad Rank score, making it easier to get to position number one in the search results for less spend.

I will show you each element of an advertisement first, as this is such a crucial part of the process, then go on to the other factors that you need to be aware of to monitor and improve the performance of your Google AdWords campaign that someone else is managing for you.

Key Components of a Google AdWords Advertisement

The Google AdWords advertisement below features most of the features available to advertisers. Notice how deep the advertisement is: seven lines, yet I often see advertisements with only three lines, because advertisers (or their agencies) do not know what they are doing. Why have a small box advertisement in a newsagent's window when you could have a billboard?

Features of a Google AdWords advertisement

Imagine you enter a search for "Probate Solicitor" and you are presented with the advertisement in position one above for a new legal brand that has just launched called "The Probateers".

I have numbered each of the different features within Google AdWords so that you can understand how they work. It is important to ensure that you use every available tool that Google provides for you to make your advertisement as large and effective as possible (and to keep your costs down).

1. YOUR ADVERTISEMENT HEADLINE: Your headline is split into two parts and you need to use each of them as the Probateers have done here.

> **Part 1: Specialist Probate Solicitors**
>
> **Part 2: Probateers Fixed Fee Service**

You will notice that they are using capitals at the start of each word (leading capitals) of their advertisement. This is a good thing to do because it increases the click-through rate (CTR). I know this because I have tested it ad nauseam: I have split-tested (tested the variables) the same advertisements with exactly the same wording, one with lower-case lettering and one with leading capitals, and the one with leading capitals always gets more clicks.

This is an important part of Google AdWords; it allows you to continually split-test different advertisements and different elements of a campaign, to see which performs better. It is through this split-testing that you find out what works and what doesn't. You don't have to guess: you can run live tests and your potential clients will tell you which advertisement they prefer by clicking one more than the other. This is how I found out that leading capitals work better than lower case lettering.

You now know that leading capitals throughout your advertisement increase the number of times that someone clicks on your advertisement. Why does this matter? Well, for two main reasons:

- the more clicks you receive, the more people visit your website, and the more phone calls you will receive about your services; and
- the number of clicks that your advertisement receives for each 100 times that it appears in front of people provides you with your click-through rate (CTR). Your CTR is a crucial number to monitor.

For example, if the "Probateers" advertisement here is displayed 100 times, but only clicked on 5 times, it will have a 5% CTR. The higher your CTR, the better your quality score and consequently your ad rank, as outlined in the equation earlier in the chapter.

An average CTR is in the region of 1–2%, but if you have a very good niche legal service or your advertisement content matches the search term entered by the user really closely, you can hit a CTR of 20% or more. This will give you an excellent ad rank and mean that, as in the examples above, you can reach position one at the same time as bidding less for your keywords to get to that position than your competitors will have done.

2. YOUR WEBSITE DISPLAY ADDRESS: This is not the address of the page that you are sending someone to, but the address that you choose to show to your potential clients. In other words, it is another opportunity for you to entice people to click through to your website by including the search term that your user has entered into Google.

The Probateers have opted for:

www.theprobateers.co.uk/Probate

The good part is that they have used a leading capital in the word 'Probate', but the bad part is that they have not used all of the available space. They could and should be using the word 'Solicitor' in there, as that was part of my search, for example:

www.theprobateers.co.uk/Probate-Solicitors

The more times someone sees the keywords (the search term) that they entered into Google, the higher the chances that they will click on the advertisement, which will increase the all-important CTR.

3. TELEPHONE HEADING: You should use the specific telephone extension to be used. It may not lead to a lot of activity because, in my experience, most people will still want to click the advertisement first to go to your website, but if you are targeting a local audience (which you can do – see later in this section) then a local phone number will resonate with your audience and increase CTR.

4. THE MAIN ADVERTISEMENT CONTENT: When I first started using Google AdWords in 2004, all that was available to you was title, advertisement copy and website address: four lines maximum.

Now the advertisement content is not 50% of the advertisement, as it used to be, taking up two of those original four lines, but it is still very important.

The Probateers have opted for:

> **Speak to the experts in Probate Law. No obligation enquiries. Fixed fee service.**

They have not used leading capitals all the way through, which needs correcting. I have also always found that using the word 'free' at the beginning of this part improves CTR, so I might change their content to this:

Free Call To Experts In Probate Law. No Obligation Enquiries. Fixed Fee Service.

5. CALL OUTS: 'Call-out extensions' are simple two- or three-word phrases which enable you to feature more reasons why the searcher should click on your advertisement. You should try to include keywords closely linked to the search terms that you are targeting.

6. STRUCTURED SNIPPET EXTENSIONS: These are very similar to call-out extensions, but they are used to detail the services provided. It is another chance to sell someone on to your website and increase your CTR.

7. SITELINK EXTENSIONS: These are one of the more important types of extensions, as they provide you with four more chances to obtain a click-through to your website, by providing links to four other related pages. The key word is 'related'. You need to link to pages that are related to the main page that you are targeting, in this case 'probate'.

Here are the Probateers sitelink extensions:

What Is Probate?	Free Probate Quote
Probate Lawyers	Client Reviews

I would ensure that each of them included the word 'probate', so would change 'Client Reviews to 'Probate Reviews. You might thing that this is overkill, but again, I have tested this and it makes a difference, so it should be done as it will increase CTR.

There is a relatively new element, 'Message Extensions', which allows you to include a telephone number so that someone can text you on their mobile or tablet directly from the results screen. I even know some companies that will answer these text messages for you.

—

The beauty of all of the elements of AdWords advertisements is that you can split- test them constantly to improve their performance. This means that rather than guessing what will work, you use your potential clients to tell you what is working best for them by seeing which combinations provide the best click-through rates for you. I will talk about this more in the next section.

Your Keywords

Your keywords are the words that you feature to attract people to your website. In the example above, the words I used to find the Probateers were 'Probate Solicitors'. These are the keywords that they were targeting, which produced the advertisement for their services.

Keywords are organised into ad groups, which should be a relatively small number of keywords, in the region of 10 to 15. For example, continuing the Probateers' example, these might be:

- Probate solicitor
- Probate solicitors
- Probate solicitor fees
- Probate solicitor charges
- Probate fixed fee
- Probate solicitor costs

• How much does a solicitor charge for probate

One keyword should not be in that list above. Can you tell which one it is?

'Probate fixed fee' is the answer. The reason is that it does not include both the words 'probate' and 'solicitor', which all of the other keywords do, so the advertisement content should match the keyword being entered.

Matching content to keyword

① **Specialist Probate Solicitors – Probateers Fixed Fee Service**
② **Ad** **www.theprobateers.co.uk/Probate** ▼   0800 1234567 ③
Speak to the experts in Probate Law. No obligation enquiries. Fixed fee service. ④
⑤ Free Enquiries ~ Specialist Service ~ Dedicated Solicitor ~ Fixed Price
Services: Grant Of Probate, Full Probate Service, Initial Telephone Advice, Probate Abroad ⑥

⑦   **What Is Probate?**   **Free Probate Quote**
                   Probate Lawyers   **Client Reviews**

In the advertisement above, to make it work better for the keyword 'probate fixed fee' I would amend the first part of it to include this keyword, for example:

'Fixed Fee Probate From The Probateers'

You might think that the words 'fixed fee' are already there, but putting them at the beginning, so that they are is the first thing the searcher sees, will improve CTR.

Keyword Match Types

One of the biggest mistakes that I see is people using the wrong match type for keywords. Match types are the method Google uses to determine when it should display your advertisement to searchers. Select the wrong match type and you allow Google to be very liberal when it comes to displaying your advertisements.

Here are the different match types, with Google's explanation of what they mean:

Google match types

Broad match

Broad match is the default match type that all your keywords are assigned. Ads may show on searches that include misspellings, synonyms, related searches and other relevant variations.

Example keyword: women's hats
Example search: buy ladies hats

Broad match modifier

Ads may show on searches that contain the modified term (or close variations, but not synonyms), in any order.

Symbol: +keyword
Example keyword: +women's +hats
Example search: hats for women

Phrase match

Ads may show on searches that are a phrase, and close variations of that phrase.

Symbol: 'keyword'
Example keyword: 'women's hats'
Example search: buy women's hats

Exact match

Ads may show on searches that are an exact term and close variations of that exact term.

Symbol: [keyword]
Example keyword: [women's hats]
Example search: women's hats

Negative match

Ads may show on searches without the term.

Symbol: -keyword
Example keyword: -women
Example search: baseball hats

What is important for you to know is that the first category, broad match, is the one Google defaults to. I call it the 'throw money away' keyword match type.

Let me show you an example of how using the 'broad match' match type can quickly cost you money that you shouldn't be spending, using a conveyancing solicitor looking for more instructions as an example.

Broad match keyword: 'conveyancing solicitor'

Below are examples of searches that might trigger the advertisement, and lead people to click on it, but without generating any instructions, which will cost the advertiser money.

- How do I sue my conveyancing solicitor?
- Conveyancing solicitor jobs
- Conveyancing solicitor salary

None of those searches will ever lead to instructions, so why does Google default to broad match as search type? Quite simply, it knows that it will produce a lot of clicks for you very quickly. However, Google then expects you to do the next part, which most business owners do not do, which is to add negative keywords to your campaign to prevent your advertisements showing when these types of terms are entered into the search box.

I take over a lot of Google AdWords campaigns which solicitors have been running themselves (in contravention of the law firm growth formula, remember) and the biggest problem I see is that all their keywords are using 'broad match', so they are generating a lot of clicks but not many instructions.

I quickly do two things:

- turn all broad match searches into phrase match searches; and
- add negative keywords for words that they do not want their advertisements to be shown for.

In the example above, the negative keywords I would add would be 'jobs', 'salary', and 'sue'.

Now, if someone searches for 'conveyancing solicitor salary' my client's advertisement will no longer be presented to them. Perfect.

These two tasks are vitally important, so if you are running a campaign already I suggest that you spend some time checking that you have negative keywords running and that you are not using broad match search terms. The easy way to do this is to look at the 'search term' report on a regular basis (ideally weekly).

On my search term report for my own AdWords Campaign:

The Google search term report

Campaign: **Samson Consulting**   Drafts ▼ Yesterday:

● Enabled   Type **Search Network only - All features** Edit   Budget: **£20.00/day** Edit   Targeting: **Ireland; UK(12 more)** Edit   Active bid adjustments: **Location, Device**

Ad Groups | **Settings** | **Ads** | **Keywords** | **Audiences** | **Dimensions** ▼

Keywords: **Negative Keywords** **Search Terms**

Segment | **Filter** | **Columns** ↓ View Change History

Search Terms
Learn how customers are finding your ad. With the Search terms report, you can see the actual searches people entered on Google Search and other Search Network sites that triggered your ad and led to a click. Depending on your keyword match types, this list might include terms other than exact matches to your keywords. Learn more

Add as keyword | Add as negative keyword

Search term	Match Type	Added/Excluded	Ad Group	Click	Impr	CTR	Avg. CPC	Cost	Converted Clicks	Avg. Pos.
Law Responsibilities For Website Design	Broad Match	None	Legal Website Design	1	1	100.00%	£1.17	£1.17	0	1.0
Legal Website Design	Exact Match	Added	Legal Website Design	1	1	100.00%	£4.94	£4.94	0	4.0
Wix Law Firm Website	Phrase Match	None	Law Firm Website Design	1	1	100.00%	£0.74	£0.74	0	6.0
Legal Marketing Services	Exact Match	Added	Legal Marketing Keywords	0	6	0.00%	£0.00	£0.00	0	1.0
Legal Marketing	Exact Match	Added	Legal Marketing Keywords	0	5	0.00%	£0.00	£0.00	0	1.2
Marketing For Law Firms	Exact Match	Added	Marketing Law Firms	0	2	0.00%	£0.00	£0.00	0	3.0
How To Win Clients Law Firm	Broad Match	None	Solicitor Clients 2	1	1	100.00%	£4.76	£4.76	0	1.0
Copyright Law	Broad Match	None	Copywriting For Solicitors	1	3	33.33%	£4.71	£4.71	0	1.0
Other Search Terms				0	296	0.00%	£0.00	£0.00	0	1.8
Total				7	318	2.20%	£3.39	£23.73	0	1.8

Let me talk you through it.

1. Choose the date range that you are looking for. I check my account regularly (almost daily) so I usually select Yesterday.

2. Select the 'Keyword' tab.

3. Select 'Search Terms', which will now show you all the search terms that actually produced a click through to your website.

4. The search term 'law responsibilities for website design uk' is not the type of search I am looking for. Therefore, I will tick the square box next to it, then select 'Add as negative keyword', importantly, I will delete all of the words except 'responsibilities', as this is the only keyword that I do not want to trigger my advertisements – with negative keywords you do want to use 'broad match' for your search criteria.

5. 'Wix law firm website'. Wix is a free website design platform that proudly states at the bottom of your website that you have a free website from Wix. It is my firm belief that no solicitor should have a free website. You are selling a professional service. What does it say about you if you won't even spend a few pounds on a website?

6. 'Copyright law' is not a search term that I want to target, so I will add this as a negative exact match, i.e. [copyright law].

By regularly looking at your search term report you will find new keywords that you can add to your campaign (Google will default to broad match, so you must ensure quotation marks are added around the keyword) and negative ones that you add to stop your advertisement being shown when unsuitable search terms are entered.

You can very quickly ensure that your AdWords manager builds you a successful campaign with good keywords simply by following these steps:

- add some modified broad match search terms for your chosen area of law, for example, '+conveyancing +solicitor';

- the checking of your search term report daily, as above, regularly adding new keywords and new negative keywords; and
- ensuring that your keywords are all in small, tightly-focused keyword groups, sending potential prospects to a well-matched landing page on your website.

Let's look at the third step.

Your Landing Pages

Ideally you should have one landing page for each Google Ad-Words ad group. Remember, I said that an ad group should have around 10–15 keywords within it, all very closely matched.

In the Probateers' example above, I suggested that one ad group might contain these keywords:

- Probate solicitor
- Probate solicitors
- Probate solicitor fees
- Probate solicitor charges
- Probate solicitor costs
- How much does a solicitor charge for probate

The landing page I would send these people to must have the keywords 'Probate Solicitor' in all the following places on that page, which will lead to a better quality score:

1. in the title tag;
2. in the description tag;
3. in the headline on the page;
4. in the opening paragraph;
5. In the 'alt' tags and 'title' tags behind the images on the page (there should always be images on the page); and
6. the content on the page (without reaching overkill – see Chapter 10).

If you have a very low quality score for a keyword, one of the most common reasons is that your landing page does not fulfil these criteria. In the example above, sending the visitor who searches for a 'probate solicitor' to a page about 'Wills, Probate and Trusts' would result in a low quality score, as the page would not match the search term closely enough, and none of the required six elements above are included.

You might say that the word 'Probate' is included, so that should be good enough, but sadly it would not be. As I say, AdWords is a science with a formula to follow. Follow that formula closely and you achieve great results. If you only half-follow it, you will get average results and spend a lot more money in the process.

Chapter 10 gave a detailed guide to all the elements of a good landing page, so I won't repeat them here, but the key point is that you must make sure that accurate keywords appear in all six locations listed above and that the content follows the formula of my content-writing for a website page.

If you are thinking that this mean you need a lot more pages on your website so you can have one for each ad group, you are right.

However, you are only changing the six elements above to match the main keywords in each ad group to create your new landing page, so it is largely a copy, paste and edit exercise. For example, while the ad group above targeted 'Probate Solicitors', the next ad group might target 'Probate Lawyers'. This definitely needs a separate landing page, but all you are going to change on that page is the word 'Solicitors' to 'Lawyers'. As I say, it's copy, paste and edit job, but one that Google will reward you for with a better-quality score, so it's time well spent.

If you know anything about search engine optimisation, you will know that Google is not a huge fan of 'duplicate content', meaning pages which by and large say almost exactly the same thing. In the probate solicitors/probate lawyers example above, both pages will be almost identical. You can quickly get round this by adding some 'behind the scenes' code that tells Google to ignore the second 'probate lawyers' page. Here is the code:

```
<meta name='robots' content='noindex'>
```

Your website developer will know where to place it, but if they don't, it needs to go in the 'head' section of your website.

Good landing pages are vital as a part of your AdWords campaign, so make sure that each AdWords group is going to a landing page that matches the search terms within that group.

Additional Techniques

As well as these core elements of a successful Google AdWords campaign, there are some other elements which are useful to know and understand.

These are found within your 'Settings' tab when you are in AdWords.

Type of campaign

Make sure you select right option here.

Once inside your Google AdWords campaign, from the central navigation select 'Settings' then 'All settings' to discover the features below.

'Search network only – All features' is the one to go for: other choices are video and the display network. My experience is that for now 'search network' is by far the most effective performer and where you should focus your efforts. Video marketing just doesn't work for law firms (sorry – legal services are just not exciting enough!), and though display marketing (banner advertising) can work to some extent, nothing beats AdWords search marketing. As most of my clients regularly exceed their set monthly budget to spend on Google AdWords, I would rather they limited themselves to having the results displayed on Google search pages only than waste money on less effective advertising.

Networks

I suggest you use only Google Search and even exclude Google Search partners. Again, in my experience, this is the most effective option. Everything else is less effective, and as most solicitors run out of budget, you need to focus on the places where you will get the best results.

Devices

Set this to 'all' to target all devices, unless you have a website which is not mobile responsive, in which case you should just choose 'desktop'. (However, refer back to Chapter 10 to see why your website *must* be mobile responsive these days.)

Location Targeting

You can choose to target geographically by choosing a whole country, town or county, or you can target within a radius of your offices, for example, 20 or 30 miles. You should select radius targeting if looking for local clients.

You should also make a selection from within the location settings.

Choosing Location Settings

Under 'Location options' select 'advanced' then under 'Target' choose 'People in, searching for or who show interest in my targeted location'.

This advanced targeting means that anyone searching or showing an interest in your area but located geographically outside of it will see your advertisements. For example, someone who works in central London but lives in Ashford, Kent, would, if they searched for an 'Ashford Solicitor' while at work, still see your advertisements even though they were not searching from your target location.

Bid Strategy

I recommend that your AdWords agency uses manual bidding (although you can select 'enhanced bidding', allowing Google to bid a little more for keywords that are converting well). The other options allow Google to set your bidding. I don't recommend this.

Budget

This is where you set your daily budget for your Google AdWords spend. If you want to spend £500 a month, divide this sum by 30 days to set your daily budget.

Delivery Method

I choose 'Accelerated' delivery. This means that your advertisements are displayed until your daily budget limit is reached. See 'budget tipping point' later, on how to over-ride this if you can afford to.

Advanced Settings

OPTIONS IN 'ADVANCED SETTINGS'

Schedule

You can schedule advertisements to run at different times of the day or to exclude weekends, but I suggest you let your advertisements run 24/7 at first. If you consistently find that your advertisements do not work on Sunday from 7 PM you could change this, but my experience suggests that you will lose instructions that you would otherwise have received.

In addition to this, by not running all the time you will miss clicks, and your overall quality score may well be lower as you keep dipping in and out of the market, making it harder to achieve consistent results.

Ad delivery, ad rotation

My Google representative always wants me to let Google rotate my advertisements to optimise conversions. She tells me that Google knows best and so I should let them run the advertisements that convert more visitors into people filling in enquiry forms. It is a good theory, but whenever I have done this I have not seen any improvement in volume or quantity that makes me believe Google controls this process better than a human.

I always choose 'rotate indefinitely' for my own and my clients' advertisements so that I can see, manually, which advertisements are working best, by which I mean which advertisements have the highest CTR. Once I know that, I can pause the worst advertisement and rewrite a new one to try to beat the current best performer's CTR. More on this shortly.

Your Role in an AdWords Campaign

Now that you know the basic elements of a campaign, how do you manage an agency running a campaign for you? What do you need to do to check that they are doing a good job for you?

Well, the beauty is that AdWords really is a numbers game. At a glance, you can see not only how well AdWords is performing, but more importantly, how many clients you have generated and how much that has produced for you in terms of fees.

Tracking Your Numbers

You absolutely must track your numbers; remember, what gets measured gets better. If you do not know how much work and how much income are being generated by an AdWords campaign, how can you know if you should keep on doing it? Quite simply, you can't.

So you must definitely measure the returns from your Google AdWords campaign. You should be looking for a minimum of a 3 to 1 return on your investment, so if you spend £1,000 a month, you want it to generate at least £3,000 in fees. If you can start at that point, you can improve that return over time as your AdWords campaign matures and improves. I have clients that regularly exceed a 10 to 1 return on investment.

Obviously, some legal matters bring in fees faster, so you have to consider your cash flow, but if you can start at a 3 to 1 return on investment, you will be making money and you should continue to run your AdWords campaign.

Two things need restating here:

- You need to ask every new prospect how they found you so that you can trace it back to your AdWords campaign. Will your receptionist do this properly? In my experience, no, which is why I recommend that you use a call centre that will ensure their staff ask the question and complete an enquiry form for each call they handle. This will enable you to measure the return from your AdWords campaign accurately. You can even use a different telephone number on your website and only divert those calls to the call centre, as a starting point to test the process out.
- You must track these enquiries through to conversion. Of course, you will be doing this already, having read Chapter 4, but when it comes to AdWords, it is vital. You must know your numbers. If you are spending £1,000 a month, how much is it making you? If you are spending £5,000 a month (yes, some solicitors do), then you have to know that it is working for you. If you are spending over £10,000 a month (yes, many solicitors do, and more too) then you have to know that it is providing you with a return on investment.

If your immediate reaction was to flinch when seeing the numbers above, I believe that will be for one of two reasons.

- You are a smaller firm and are barely billing more than £10,000 a month, so spending that amount would bankrupt you. Don't worry; you wouldn't need to spend that much. If you are in this position and are looking to move from being a £10,000-a-month firm to a £20,000-a-month firm then your spend will probably need to be between £1,000 to £1,500 to make this happen.
- Until now, you have never really measured the returns from your marketing, so the thought of spending that much money on any aspect of it scares you. Now that you have the law firm growth formula in your hands, though, this is going to change – if you are serious about growing your law firm, that is. A serious law firm owner knows their current position, where they want

to be, and they measure every single step of the journey to reach their destination.

Remember that there is a simple spreadsheet that you can use to track your numbers contained in the resources at www .samsonconsulting.co.uk/growth; it will be more than enough to get you started. You don't need to add features that you will never need to your case management system (CMS). I have never seen a CMS that was actually up to any marketing task. They are one-trick ponies, so leave them to do their usual trick and use a spreadsheet to do the rest to start with.

Measure Your Performance

If your first job is to measure the return from your spend, your second job is to measure the AdWords campaign performance figures and to keep on top of your AdWords provider to ensure that these numbers keep on working in your favour.

So, what do these numbers look like? Let's take a look at a simple Google AdWords report showing the core numbers. These are my own numbers; not surprisingly, my clients like to keep their numbers to themselves, but the only thing that is important is for you to see the numbers, so I can explain what questions you should be asking and what results you should be expecting.

There is actually a simple lesson within a lesson here. You see, I know that some of my competitors will buy and read this book. They will see my figures below and believe that having this information will enable them to do exactly what I do to generate a lovely client book of really nice law firm owners. It doesn't worry me. They might have some baseline figures, but that's all they know. They can't see or hear the conversations that I have with my clients or the private emails we send. Generally, I find, a lot of law firm owners are scared or even terrified of sharing information with one another. In my experience, sharing usually only leads to mutual benefits, so I strongly urge you to share away.

Here is a chart showing my last few months' activity on Google AdWords:

Google Adword reporting

Month	Clicks	Impr.	CTR	Avg.CPC	Cost	Avg. position	All conv.
February	183	6,754	2.71%	£3.28	£599.77	1.7	17
January	271	10,173	2.66%	£3.67	£993.26	1.7	4
December	192	7,215	2.66%	£3.70	£710.36	1.7	21
November	348	20,068	1.73%	£3.13	£1,090.79	2.1	30
October	329	16,466	2%	£2.59	£851.20	2.4	37
September	158	5,241	3.01%	£2.85	£449.99	1.7	21
August	117	5,156	2.27%	£3.75	£439.16	1.6	11
July	118	6,897	1.71%	£3.54	£417.53	1.5	7

If I was managing myself as a supplier – and I do – here are the questions that I would want to be asking.

Q Why did the average position of my advertisement drop from 1.7 to 2.4 in October?

Remember, there are four AdWords spaces available at the top of the search results. I want to be in position one more often than not. In my case, above, I know it was because in those two months I experimented with a lot more keywords, which is why I also spent more. But if you are not in average positions 1 or 2, you need to find out why and ask your AdWords people to work to make that happen. How? As detailed above, it is all down to the ad rank formula.

SMALL KEYWORD GROUPS: Another reason why my average position might have changed is if my keywords were not in small, tightly-connected ad groups. Are they in groups of 10 to 15 keywords? If there are many more, keep the 10 or 15 that are most closely matched and start a new ad group that covers the new keywords.

In my example, there are 13 keywords within the ad group, so I am not breaking any of my own rules (phew).

Here are a few of them, so that you can follow the thread.

Key words on an ad group

Keyword
[marketing for law firms]
[marketing for law firms uk]
"marketing law firm"
[marketing a law firm]
[marketing law firms]
[law marketing]

The main keyword is 'marketing', and the word 'law firm' also appears, so I need to bear this in mind when looking at the next two parts.

SPLIT-TESTING ADVERTISEMENTS: – Are your suppliers regularly split-testing the advertisement copy to see what works best, then rewritingthe copy that doesn't work so well? Here is an example of me split-testing two advertisements against each other, so you can see how this looks within AdWords:

Split-testing advertisements

Ad	Click	Impr	CTR	Avg. CPC	Cost	Avg. Pos.
Marketing Law Firms in The UK Solicitor (Non-Practising) [Ad] www.Samsonconsulting.co.uk/Marketing-Law/Firms-UK ▼ Free Guide Shares 6 Most Effective Marketing Methods For Law Firms In The UK.	20	368	5.43%	£3.67	£73.47	1.5
Marketing Law Firms In The UK Solicitor (Non-Practising) [Ad] www.Samsonconsulting.co.uk/Marketing-Law/Firms-UK ▼ Free Guide Shares 6 Most Effective Marketing Methods for Law Firms In The UK	1	44	2.27%	£4.13	£4.13	1.5

Both advertisements feature the core keywords of 'law firm' and 'marketing', which is crucial.

You can see that one advertisement is achieving a CTR of 5.43%

(5.43 clicks through to my site for every 100 times it has been shown – Impr, or impressions). This is clearly beating the advertisement that I am running against it. However, notice that the second advertisement has only been shown 44 times, so I will leave it to run until it has been shown at least 100 times, but usually between 500 to 1000 times. This is a big enough test volume to prove that what you are seeing is not just a fluke.

You should also run through this same process with your sitelink, call-out and snippet extensions, as increasing CTRs for these extensions also improves your overall performance, quality score, and ad rank and lowers costs. I won't go through every one of these, as it is exactly the same process as for changing your main advertisement content, but I wanted to ensure that you look at them too.

LANDING PAGE REVIEW: Does the landing page that your prospects are being sent to closely match the search terms entered? Continuing my example above, here is the content from the page that people clicking one of my two advertisements are sent to:

The 6 Fastest Ways For Solicitors To Win New Clients

UK Law Firm Marketing Guide For Solicitors Looking to Double Or Treble Their Turnover.

If you would like to know the six most effective methods for solicitors to grow their law firms, alongside the formula to follow to allow you to do this whilst still running the day to day delivery of legal services, this book is for you.

The 6 Fastest Ways For Solicitors To Attract New Clients has been downloaded by over 5,000 solicitors across the UK and I have received many emails thanking me for helping solicitors to finally start to get to grips with their...

Nick Jervis
Solicitor (non-practising)

How could this page be improved? Look at it with a totally critical eye and make a note of a few things that could be changed to make it match the keywords and advertisements in question better.

Now let me show you the revised page and talk you through the changes.

The 6 Most Effective Methods For Law Firms To Win New Clients

The Law Firm Marketing Guide For Solicitors Looking to Double Or Treble Their Turnover.

If you would like to know the six most effective methods for solicitors to grow their law firms, alongside the formula to follow to allow you to do this whilst still running the day to day delivery of legal services, this book is for you.

The 6 Fastest Ways For Solicitors To Attract New Clients has been downloaded by over 5,000 solicitors across the UK and I have received many emails thanking me for helping solicitors to finally start to get to grips with their...

Nick Jervis, Solicitor And UK Law Firm Marketing Specialist

By making two simple changes – adding the keywords 'law firm' and 'marketing' to the title on the page and beneath my photograph – I have improved the relevance of the page and my quality score. This in turn will improve my ad rank and allow me to return to the top position for a lower spend than my competitors.

These are the things that you need to ask your AdWords administrator to do if you are not hitting the top position or if your costs are rising (or both).

Q Why were there only four conversions in January, compared with 21 in December and 17 in February?

Conversions represent people taking the action that you want them to take. In my case a conversion is someone completing the request for my free guide and landing on my 'thank you' page. I have placed a piece of AdWords tracking code on this page, and each time someone lands on it the code triggers a conversion.

The most common reasons for a drop in conversions could be:

- the tracking code not working (this happens quite a lot and is exactly what did happen on my website in January);
- receiving a lower number of clicks. This is not the case in my example, as there were 271 clicks for four conversions in January, compared with 183 clicks for 17 conversions in February;
- the average cost per click jumping up, either because someone else has entered my market space or my ad rank has dropped for the other reasons outlined above. Again, this is not the case with my example but I want to point out the options so that you can ask the right questions of your AdWords agency.

Q Why did the click-through rate drop in November?
The CTR rate is a really important figure, so seeing it drop in November would be a concern. However, as I mentioned above, I was experimenting with a lot of new ad groups, and with keywords that were not as focused as my usual ones. Once I had gone through this phase, the CTR went back up to figures heading towards 3%. This is an average – remember one of the CTRs above was over 5% – but watching the averages is usually enough to give you a warning that there is something amiss.

The Budget Tipping Point

It is worth mentioning what I call the 'budget tipping point'. You will often find that Google tells you that your budget is limited. If you are capping your spend at £30 a day, roughly £900 a month, Google might suggest that your campaign is 'Limited byy budget' in nice orange letters.

You can even click a chart and it will show you what might happen if you increase your daily cap, as below.

Google budget increase forecast

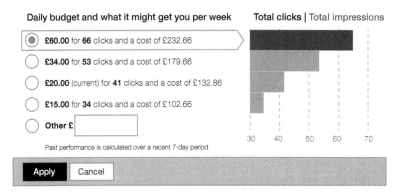

Daily budget and what it might get you per week

○ **£60.00** for **66** clicks and a cost of £232.66

○ **£34.00** for **53** clicks and a cost of £179.66

○ **£20.00** (current) for **41** clicks and a cost of £132.86

○ **£15.00** for **34** clicks and a cost of £102.66

○ Other £

Past performance is calculated over a recent 7-day period

Total clicks | Total impressions

30   40   50   60   70

Apply   Cancel

The only point I want to mention here is that if your budget is limited, in other words you are often spending more than your daily budget amount, you may well miss visitors who would turn into clients.

When you increase your budget to such an extent that you receive all available clicks (only do this when you have been running an efficient campaign for some time), then you can find that by doubling your budget you may actually receive triple the enquiries, making it even more profitable. I believe this happens because some prospects will return to your website two or three times before making contact with you, so when your budget runs out part-way through the day, these prospects do not find your advertisement or website the second or third time. Once you increase your budget, they no longer have any trouble finding you.

This, alongside the fact that everyone now searching for your keywords will find you because you are omnipresent, is why I believe that this 'budget tipping point' exists.

———

Running an AdWords campaign is a science. You cannot be expected to learn that science and run your law firm, but you can now I hope, with what is contained in this chapter, and the later chapter on optimisation, know which questions to ask to ensure that your campaign is working as hard as it possibly can for you.

Chapter 12

Marketing Artery 4: Referrals

While this is the last of the marketing arteries in this book, it is by no means the least. However, most solicitors automatically build up a good flow of new instructions from referral partners. Where they fail, in my experience, is in ensuring that they monitor accurately all referrals into their practice and reward their referral partners appropriately. The reward does not have to be a fee – it doesn't even need to be a financial reward – but the point is that there has to be some kind of reward or at some point the referrals will dry up.

I am often staggered by the arrogance of some solicitors, who believe that their referral partner should just be grateful that the solicitor is looking after their clients for them. Yes, that used to be the case, but like it or not, the world has moved onto a much more commercial footing. You know this; it is why you are reading this book. This is good news, though, because it means that those solicitors who for years have just got by through their very existence and not much else are now either struggling or their referral partners are waiting for you to come and find them.

With the right systems and processes in place, a commercially-minded and sensitive solicitor can come along and clean up. What are the systems and processes required? You need a very simple system for tracking referrals, and a process to generate more of them by building the relationship with your referrer and rewarding them.

Your Referral Tracking System

All you really need is a spreadsheet tracking all referrals into your practice and including the name of your referral partner(s). There is one in the resources section at www.samsonconsulting.co.uk /growth.

Most solicitors confirm to me that referrals make up a good proportion of their new client instructions – often as much as 50%. However, when I ask them how they measure this and how they reward their referral partners, they look back at me with a blank face.

The importance of reciprocating

One firm was receiving around 50 conveyancing instructions every month from a firm of financial advisers. The advisers knew this because they kept track of them. One month they sat down with the solicitors and said 'We are sending you 50 new clients a month. What can you do to help our business?' The solicitors replied 'Well, we don't really get the opportunity to refer work back to you, and we are not going to pay you for the referrals, so there is nothing we can do.' That was that. The financial advisers placed their referrals elsewhere.

They would have been happy with an attempt by the solicitors to generate referrals back to their firm, but of course the law firm did not have an email marketing database, never kept in touch with its clients, and failed to see why they should make the effort in the first place.

So, even at a conservative estimate of the fee levels, £25,000 of income per month (50 × £500) disappeared overnight.

You have to be commercially minded when it comes to referrals or you will lose out, just like this firm did.

If referrals are important to your law firm, which they should be, you must take responsibility for tracking them and for ensuring that your referral partners are happy.

I often find that just going through the process of tracking all referrals into a practice is a real eye opener for a solicitor. They suddenly realise that the firm they thought of as their best referrer is actually not their best referrer, and one which they thought was referring a client now and again is sending them far more business than that.

Once you really know who is referring the most business to you each month, you can ensure that they are happy with your relationship and work on improving it.

Your Referral Improvement Process

There are two ways to achieve more referrals:

- get more referrals from existing referral partners; and
- find more referral partners.

Obtaining More Referrals from Existing Referral Partners

Once you are measuring who is referring to you and how many clients they are referring, you suddenly know where you need to spend your time.

If someone is already a regular referrer, spend more time with them. Find out how you can help them, not just with the aim of receiving more referrals from them, but with a genuine interest in helping them because they are helping you. Reciprocation is crucial.

Whenever you are considering referrals, remember my Triangle of mutual benefit, as shown below:

Triangle of mutual benefit

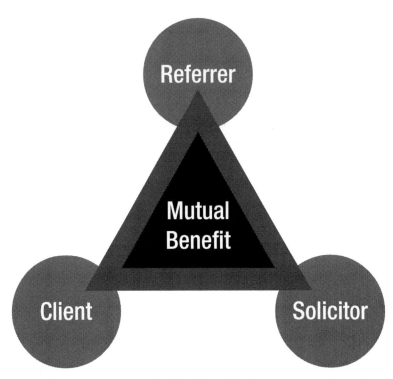

Unless everyone involved in the referral process receives a benefit from it, it simply won't work. Well, it might work once, but it won't produce the steady and consistent law firm growth that you are trying to achieve here.

Suppose someone refers a client to you: the client must benefit by being referred to a great service provider and receiving a great service, the referrer must benefit because you must refer to them reciprocally or thank them in some other meaningful way, and you will benefit from receiving a new client with very little effort on your part.

If you fail to reward those who are referring to you, or you fail to provide a great service for the client, there is no 'mutual benefit' to support the triangle so it collapses, leading to a flat line...

What starts off as a little flurry of activity from the referral soon goes flat if the referrer isn't thanked or the client receives a poor service. The referral relationship is dead. You have flatlined.

STEP 1 – ASK THE REFERRER WHAT THEY WANT! How do you find out how to get from A to B on a journey? You ask someone or you ask Google Maps.

You find out what your referral partner would like from your relationship in exactly the same way. When you ask them, you can be as straight-talking or as gentle as you like, whichever is your natural style, but ask them you must if you want the relationship to prosper. You will receive one of the following answers (or a combination of them).

Some referrers will be perfectly happy with a good, open working relationship with you. If this is the answer you receive, make sure they mean it. Ask them if there is anything else you can do to make the relationship better. If they still feel this way, make a diary note to sit down and review the relationship with them again, and possibly pop something in the post to them as a thank-you. This can be something as simple as a postcard, a thank-you note, some flowers or wine.

Other referrers may say that they are happy referring to you, but that they would appreciate more updates from you about the client matter so that they know what is going on. Make sure that you set up a system for updating them and ask them how they would like to receive the updates (by email, post or telephone call).

Another option is that the referrer asks for referrals back to their business, and why shouldn't they? After all, if they are supporting your business, why shouldn't you do the same for them? If they have clients that need your services, then nine times out of ten your clients will also have a need for their services from time to time.

'But Nick, where am I going to get these referrals from?' I hear you say. There are two easy ways:

- the same way that they generate referrals for your business;: by talking to your clients about them in face-to-face meetings; and

- by including in your email newsletter content from your referral partner that will be of interest to your client base. .

In both of these situations it is vital that you keep control of the referral, so that you can measure how many referrals you are sending back to your referral partner. Therefore, if your client expresses interest in their services in a face-to-face meeting, you make the introduction by email after the meeting and add the details to your 'referrals out' tab.

If you include content from them in your email newsletter, do not provide the contact details but ask clients to reply to your email if they would like their contact details, then again you make the introduction and add them to your 'referrals out' tab.

Finally, some referrers will say that they expect you to pay them. Whether you do this, or can legally do this, is clearly up to you. If none of the options above can be made to work (most of them can), then it is an option, but it would always be my preference to work on one of these options or a combination of them. Financial referrals tend to go only one way and that is up.

STEP 2 – ASK HOW YOU CAN GENERATE MORE REFERRALS: The second part of this process should only take place once you have gone through the process above for a few months. If you dive straight into this part of the process, you will alienate some of your existing referral partners. You need to remember my marketing mantra 'Clients First' and apply that to your referrer in this case.

Step 1 is all about ensuring that your referral partner is happy with your relationship and is receiving mutual benefit in some way, shape or form. If you dive straight to step 2, they will realise that you are only interested in getting more from them without doing anything in return. You will flatline the relationship.

However, once you have put in place a system of mutual benefit and run it for a few months, knowing that you are both very happy with it, it is perfectly acceptable to ask how you can 'amplify' the referrals, as it will benefit both of your businesses.

Once again, a simple face-to-face meeting is the ideal way to do this.

STEP 3 – DO A CROSS-PROMOTION EVENT: Once you have an email marketing database (see Chapter 9), you have a never- ending opportunity to support your referral partners, as you can offer to promote any seminars or webinars that they are putting on, and in return ask them to do the same for any seminars or webinars that you are running.

This is such a softly-softly yet highly effective strategy, as long as when you are running a seminar or webinar, you ensure that everyone attending registers through your email marketing database so that you can keep in touch with them indefinitely, until they instruct you.

Solicitors

Other firms of solicitors are often some of my clients' best referrers. If you operate in a niche, approaching other solicitors who do not provide the services that you provide can lead to regular referrals.

The same triangle of mutual benefit rules apply in that they must receive something from you, too. However, if you are sending a regular email newsletter, you can mention their services to your clients to generate reciprocal referrals – which also gives you something else to talk about in your newsletter.

―

This isn't a long chapter, because most solicitors are very good at starting referral relationships, but less so at keeping them going. I have provided you with a formula to follow to ensure that this is not the case for you. Measure your referrals, ensure that there is mutual benefit for the referral partner, then ask for more referrals from them.

When you have been through this process a few times, you will know exactly what each type of referrer would like to receive from you by way of mutual benefit. If you find you are not receiving as many referrals as you would like, you can approach other potential referral partners knowing exactly what is likely to make them want to refer clients to you.

Chapter 13

Your Marketing Capillaries

You are now armed with the four marketing arteries from the preceding chapters. You should be starting with these if you want to grow. If you do not have all four in place, start by putting one of them in place first, before you work your way through this chapter. If you do have all four in place, I recommend that you also work through the optimisation checklists featured in Chapter 14.

Once you have done that, you can look at the other forms of marketing covered in this Chapter, but bear in mind that these are more from the 'elephant marketing' camp than the 'peacock marketing' camp. That is not to say that they cannot be made to work for you; they can; but it is just that it is normally faster and more cost effective to start with the marketing arteries.

Advertising

Most solicitors spend several hundred pounds a month on advertising, either in local magazines, in papers or in niche publications. When I ask how these advertisements are performing, I am usually met with a blank gaze. As with all marketing, you need to know if it is working, or whether you should stop doing it.

Those few hundred pounds a month would be much better spent securing your client base with a monthly email newsletter or promoting your website using Google AdWords.

However, if you are advertising, following my PASTOR copywriting formula (see below) will ensure that you get a good response.

A PASTOR advertisement does *not* look like the one below, whereas nearly every advertisement for a solicitor that I see does:

Standard advertisement

The usual format is:

- Logo at top
- List of services
- Contact details

Remember that advertising is a form of interruption marketing, so you have to stop your prospect from reading the publication and get them to take note of your advertisement instead.

Sadly, your firm's logo and business name, while very important to you or me, really don't matter a jot to your clients. All they are interested in is their life and any problems they have at this moment. Therefore, you need to hit the nail on the head as far as they are concerned and start by addressing a problem that they might currently be facing.

Let's look at my PASTOR copywriting formula in action:

P – **Problem**

A – **Agitate**

S – **Solution**

T – **Travel**

O – **Offer**

R – **Rally**

Problem

The brain reacts to problems. It is easiest to see how this works by looking at an example of an advertisement.

Whereas, as we have seen in the advertisement above, most will start with the firm's name, a PASTOR advertisement starts by jumping up and down and saying to the prospect 'Look, this advertisement is for you...'

'Are you sure your children will be properly provided for?'

Now if I do have a family, that headline is going to at least get me to read the next line, isn't it?

I need to stress a point here. The headline of your advertisement is the *most* important part of your advertisement bar none!

The headline of your advertisement is the *most* important part of your advertisement bar none!

If you fail to spend enough time on the headline, the rest of your efforts will be completely and utterly wasted. You need to decide who your target audience is, and then write an advertisement that talks to them and them alone. In the example above, if you try and write for clients who do not have children, you will weaken the impact. To have impact you must highlight a problem or a concern for your target 'ideal' client.

Now let's move on to the next stage of my PASTOR system: 'agitating' the problem...

Agitate

The purpose of the agitate section is to expand on the headline. The headline needs to 'grab' the reader's attention, the agitation section needs to expand that headline and make it clear that this advertisement is definitely talking to them and that they need to keep reading on.

'Did you know that if you fail to leave a Will, your wishes for the guardianship of your children may not be taken into account?'

Solution

Now we need to introduce our solution, gently at first.

'A professionally drafted Will ensures that your wishes for the guardianship of your children are properly taken into consideration.'

Travel

The PASTOR copywriting formula then takes the advertisement to the next level, allowing you to expand on how you can help your target audience, which will hugely increase the chances of them picking up the telephone and asking for your help.

'While we accept that making a Will is not inherently exciting, the peace of mind it can provide you with when it comes to your wishes for the future protection of your children cannot be quantified in terms of monetary value.'

Offer

You now need to provide your potential client with an offer to contact you.

> 'For a limited time only, and for the first 20 people to reply, we are offering a Will with free storage for life in our fireproof and waterproof safe.'

You may already offer free storage, but I can guarantee that your clients will *not* know this, and if they are thinking of making a Will, the next worry is 'Where am I going to put it when I've got it?' By including this as an 'offer', you are enhancing the value of your service in the mind of your prospects.

You will note I have mentioned that this offer is limited to only 20 people. This is important, as you need to create scarcity in your client's mind to ensure that they take action, especially when it comes to Wills. It needs to be a genuine offer (you can't keep running this every week), but with a little imagination you can change the offer.

My advice is that the offer should never be price based (which devalues your core service) but 'value added' instead.

Rallying call to action

Everyone is incredibly busy and everyone has a limited budget. You need to make the effort to create urgency; your advertisement may catch your prospective client's eye and they may be interested in your service, but unless they take action your advertisement will not make you any profit.

'This offer is limited to the first 20 people to reply and is only available during [insert month]. To ensure you are one of the first to reply, please call us free now 0800 XXXXX and ask for Melanie Jones to find out more, but remember to do so by [date].'

If you follow this formula you will create advertisements that stand out from the majority of the other advertisements in your chosen publication, but, more importantly, they will make your telephone ring and instructions will follow.

Direct Mail

Direct mail can be particularly effective in the context of business-to-business services. If you know that you receive a lot of instructions from a certain type of business or a certain business sector, somebody out there can supply you with the contact data for other companies that match your current client base.

If you create a well-crafted letter, with an offer and a deadline (using the PASTOR copywriting formula from the preceding section), then follow up that letter with a telephone call (outsourced, of course) you will achieve success. I have had clients spend several hundred pounds to win tens of thousands worth of pounds of instructions using direct mail.

You can use exactly the same formula to target referral partners who are similar to your current referral partners. You will know more about their needs and wants when you have gone through the process in Chapter 12.

Selling a Service That Is Not Required Instantly

I sell one of these services, so I understand this point well. If you sell a service which does not provide an instant scratch for someone's itch, such as employment law services for employers, your offer must involve providing something of value in exchange for your potential client's permission to keep in touch with them – bearing in mind that most companies already have a solicitor and will only change them when they are sufficiently frustrated with their service.

In my case, I provide *The 6 Fastest Ways for Solicitors to Attract New Clients* as a free download. Once someone has downloaded this guide, they will hear from me every week until they either ask me to help them or they unsubscribe. I have already mentioned that the average time between a solicitor downloading my guide and asking me to help them is two years, so you will understand why this is a crucial part of my business.

Now I know that you will be thinking that sending out emails once a week is too frequent, but the point is that you must offer something to your clients in exchange for their email details, and then you must send something out consistently. Otherwise, what will happen is that at the point when they do decide to change their solicitor, you won't be the only solicitor that they contact to talk about moving over to you.

In my employment example above, you might offer a guide with this title:

How to Dismiss Any Employee Legitimately Within Six Months.

The crucial point is that it has to answer a problem that they have now or that they might have in the future. If you do not want to provide a written guide, using direct mail to promote a live webinar on the topic in question is another smart thing to do to get permission to speak with more of your prospects. It is a very gentle 'try before you buy' offer, but one that allows your clients to see that you really are an expert in your field of law.

Remember when presenting a webinar to make the content all about your clients: 'Clients First'. Do not talk too much about the law, but just about how it impacts your audience and what action they should take to protect themselves. This is all that they are interested in hearing about, and if you present your webinar in these terms you will set yourself above your competition.

Networking

I know that a lot of solicitors spend a lot of time networking. I am not certain it is always productive, but now that you have worked through Chapter 3 you should be able to present the benefits of using your firm well to anyone at these events.

My only comment about networking is that it must serve one of two purposes;

- it must provide a return on investment; or
- it must provide you with a mental boost, or ideas from other business owners that you can implement in your own business.

If it is not doing either of these things, should you be doing so much of it?

Social Media

When you see a toddler playing, or a young puppy, they have one thing in common. Give them something new and shiny to play with and they will play with it for a good 10 or 15 minutes like it is the best thing on the planet. After that 10- or 15-minute period, they move onto the next shiny new thing, then the next, and on it goes.

I am still utterly amazed that so many people believe that 'social media' is that new shiny object. If I had a £1 for every time a solicitor talks to me for the first time and, after having explained that they are desperate for some new client instructions, they suggest to me that they feel that social media is their answer. Let me tell you that the only time that social media is the answer is in response to this question:

> Q_How can I spend a huge amount of time and a fair amount of money in the sure and certain knowledge that it will be practically impossible for me to get a return on my investment?
>
> A Social media.

I have given social media its own section because I know that so many people reading this book will be thinking that it is something that they should be spending more time and money on. Why do they feel this? Why do so many educated, intelligent people believe that social media can ever be the answer to the 'not having enough clients' question?

Think about what social media really is: the sharing of exciting/glamorous/fun information in photo or text format. That is all it is.

So, if that is what social media is all about, please explain to me where the excitement, glamour or fun comes from in relation to the law? Sadly, and I hate to be the one to break this to you, but the law just isn't any of these things.

It is not like buying a new dress and showing it to all of your family and friends, or posting that cute kitten video to get a million shares. Can you imagine this in relation to a legal scenario? 'Thanks to all the team @lawfirm for the most amazing divorce. It was such fun #brokenandbattered.' Or 'Amazing effort from everyone @lawfirm. I may have suffered severe injuries which leave me in pain every single day, but at least I now have some compensation.'

I have made this point as bluntly as I can because I don't want you to fall into the traps set by all these marketing faddists who survive by selling the next big thing to unsuspecting people.

I asked why so many solicitors believe that social media is the answer and it is all because of these people selling the next big thing. The funny part is that you will notice if you have been asked to invest in some social media training recently, or to outsource your social media to a company to do it all for you, that nine times out of ten they approach you by spam emailing you, not by using social media.

Surely if social media is that good they would reach you by using social media, wouldn't they? It just proves my point. I hope I have made it sufficiently strongly to you.

How You Should Use Social Media in Your Marketing

There are two bona fide uses for social media for your law firm.

1. LINKING BACK TO NEW CONTENT ON YOUR WEBSITE: Every time you add new content to your website (see Chapter 10) you should post a comment and a link back to that content on your website. This way, Google knows that your website is being updated, and occasionally, if you are commenting on a very topical subject, you might get a few extra visitors to your website.

To do this, I use Hootsuite, which allows me to post to all of my social media networks from just one piece of software, so it means I get the message out there without having to post it separately on Facebook, LinkedIn and Twitter.

2. LINKEDIN: You should have a decent profile on LinkedIn that accurately reflects who you are and the service that your firm provides. Use the process contained in Chapter 3 to summarise in your profile why anyone should choose to work with you/your firm and spend some time connecting with your clients (if you are in the business-to-business market). However, do not spend hours on LinkedIn thinking that it will be your salvation. It will not. The marketing arteries will be, so focus your time and energy on those.

Other Marketing Capillaries

There are of course other methods for marketing your law firm. You can use videos (helpful, but not going to single-handedly transform your practice) or press coverage (this usually follows automatically when you create a great website with unique content), but these alone will not produce a steady and consistent flow of new clients for you.

I want you to focus on the marketing tactics that will, based on my far too many years of experience, actually put more money into your bank account than they will take out of it and will do so consistently. The four marketing arteries are your starting point; the capillaries contained in this chapter are useful, but only once you have fully implemented and then optimised (see Chapter 14) each of the marketing arteries.

Chapter 14

Optimisation

> 'What is the secret to successfully and continually attracting more clients to my law firm?'

The answer is just one word, is very dull, is not the next big thing, and requires a little bit of time and effort: optimisation. What does this mean? According to the *Oxford English Dictionary*, optimisation is 'the action of making the best or most effective use of a situation or resource: "companies interested in the optimisation of the business"'. Optimisation is my favourite word, and it should be yours too.

The good news is that if you continually optimise all your marketing so that it works better and better all the time, you will reach what Malcolm Gladwell calls in his excellent book of the same name, 'the tipping point'. This is the point at which all of the hard work and effort that you have put in over a period of time begins to deliver amazing results for you. More clients start calling you, filling in your website enquiry forms, replying to your email newsletter asking for information about your services, clicking on your Google AdWords, and you receive more referrals from known businesses and acquaintances.

What happens when you optimise is that everything gradually

gets better until it all works swimmingly well and delivers new client after new client to your door. But if you don't take the time to optimise, you leave an awful lot of 'free money' on the floor. Failing to optimise means that you let tens or hundreds of thousands of pounds' worth of instructions slip through your fingers. This is 'easy win' money as well, because optimising is largely about tweaking what you are already doing to make it better, as opposed to spending a lot more money on a new marketing tactic.

Simple changes can produce incredible results. The beauty of many of these changes (and I will go into the best ones shortly) is that once you make them, in many cases they keep on generating new clients for you every month thereafter, so it is time well spent.

Here are some examples of what optimisation can do, based on real marketing results for my clients.

- An email newsletter that had previously produced no tangible results suddenly made the telephone ring regularly when it was sent out every month without fail.
- An old referral source that had completely dried up was restored by two or three direct contacts over a two- to three-month period.
- A direct mail campaign that produced virtually no results became a hugely successful one generating tens of thousands of pounds' worth of instructions by adding follow-up calls to the process.
- Doubling the budget of a Google AdWords campaign almost tripled its results.
- A website producing no instructions instantly turned into one producing daily instructions by adding consistent calls to action to each page.

These results are not one-offs. They are results that I have achieved time and time again for my clients by drilling into the detail of the marketing they are currently doing or that they have done in the past but then stopped, then restarting and optimising these activities until they produce dramatically better results.

You can achieve the same results by working through these optimisation checklists and applying the changes to your own marketing.

You can download the optimisation checklists from www .samsonconsulting.co.uk/growth.

Website optimisation checklist

1.	Have you followed the overall design template contained in Chapter 10.
2.	Do you specify what you do? Does the word 'Solicitor(s)' appear immediately below your logo?
3.	Does your home page design allow people to get from there to the following as quickly as possible: • Your main services • Your contact page • Your enquiry form • Your 'about us' page
4.	Are there engaging headlines on each page?
5.	Copywriting – do you fall into the EAMWDYTOM trap, or have you managed to put your Clients First in all of your content? (EAMWDYTOM = Enough About Me, What Do You Think Of Me? i.e. talking all about yourself and not the client?)
6.	What is it you want me to do? Is there a strong call to action at the bottom of every page, giving me the telephone number, email address and a link to the free enquiry form?
7.	Are all telephone numbers hyperlinked so people can click to call from their computer or phone? Here is the code your designer needs: <a href='tel:01275855525'>01275 855525</a>)
8.	Are you following the two-minute trust builder? **Depth of expertise** • Are there enough pages per area of law served (5 to 10 minimum)? • Is there sufficient depth of content on each page (400 words minimum)? **Proof of expertise (external endorsements)** • Specialist qualifications – you don't have to have them, but if you do, publicise them and link to the 'proof of expertise' (see the website design wireframe in Chapter 10) explaining what they mean –never link to the website of the logo/endorsement). • Reviews/testimonials • Press coverage. If you have it, display the logos and link to your 'proof of expertise'. • Books/articles published (logos of magazines/journals again linking to 'proof of expertise' page) • How many people have you helped to date?

9.	Enquiry form – 60% of your visitors want this. Do you have it and is it easily accessible from every page? It should never be on your contact page (too confusing); it should have its own page.
10.	Navigation: KISS test – keep it simple… • Alphabetical • Expands when you dive deeper into an area of law • Is on the top and left, or top only (top and left works best) • Is never on the right-hand side (which is where your form or the link to your enquiry form should be). People read in an 'F' pattern, so navigation just doesn't work here, no matter what your website designer says.
11.	No prices displayed. The purpose of your website is to sell the first contact. Adding prices simply leads to you being used as a price comparison point.
12.	Have you broken up the copy (dual readership path) with • headings? ❑ • subheadings? ❑ • images? ❑ • bullet points? ❑ • videos? ❑
13.	Do you have reviews on every page and one main page of reviews – and add to them continually? Stop at 6000, not 6.
14.	Are your case studies easily accessible? ('Oh, great, you helped someone else just like me so you must be able to help me too…')
15.	Do you have free guides/reports/discussion papers available for high value/ niche topics? These may not even be downloaded but they prove your expertise.
16.	Do you have live chat or automated live chat?
17.	Do you have an 'about us' page? (It doesn't matter whether it's business or individual services, people buy people, and this is one of the most visited pages on a website). Make sure it includes • pictures ❑ • friendly content ❑ • interesting content. ❑
18.	Do you add at least two new pieces of quality content to your website every month?
19.	Do you regularly 'optimise' your best website pages? Look at your most visited pages (look at Behaviour/Site Content/All Pages in Google Analytics) and improve the content, images, and call to action to generate more enquiries from people who have found your website. Make a diary note to do this once a quarter.

Email Newsletter Optimisation Checklist

1.	Do you send it every month without fail? If you already send one every month, could you send it fortnightly?
2.	Do you regularly 'split-test' subject lines to improve open rates, or does it always say 'Smithers Jones Latest Newsletter', which will lead to reduced open rates.
3.	If you send one with images, have you tested sending an email that is content rich only, without any graphics? Email providers often strip out graphics, so your email may display very badly if you have included many images.
4.	If you send content-only emails, have you tried sending an email with images? The astute among you will recognise that this is the opposite to what I said above – the point is that the only way to find out what works best for you is to test!
5.	Have you tried different formats for your email, for example, • including a full article in the email? ❑ • including a heading and the first few sentences then linking to the full article on your website? ❑ • including case studies or reviews or feedback from referral sources who think you are wonderful? ❑ • making offers for your legal services? Yes, I mean actually asking for the instruction. ❑ • including a postscript to highlight a new service or a new offer? • including some personal stories? Staff updates, your team's hobbies, fundraising – it is all about people, so the more rapport you can build, the better. ❑ • following the PASTOR copywriting formula for any offers you make? ❑ • including a list of your core services at the end of each email?
6.	Do you add every prospect/potential referrer to your email database, regardless of whether they instruct you? (If you don't, you should – why have only one chance of winning the business when you can create 12 every year?)
7.	Are you making the EAMDYTOM mistake featured at number 5 in the website checklist?

Referrals and recommendations optimisation checklist

1.	Do you record every referral that you make and receive? If not, you must do so in order that you can reward your referral partners properly and also track your referrals to other businesses to make sure they reward you.
2.	Do you communicate with your referrers at least once a month?
3.	Do you reward your good inbound referral partners regularly?
4.	Do you work on building the relationship with those that refer clients to you sporadically, so that they refer more clients?
5.	Do you track your referrals to other solicitors and other businesses?
6.	Do you follow up to see how the referral progressed? (This has the dual benefit of having more contact with the person you have sent new business to, and reminding them that you are referring to them and that they should be doing more for you.)
7.	However you currently communicate with your partners, could you add more methods, including: • thank-you cards/postcards? ☐ • gifts? ☐ • lunches/dinners? ☐ • festive treats? ☐ • press clippings of articles of interest? ☐
8.	Have you looked for new referral partners?
9.	Think about how you found your current best referrers. Can you do more of the same to find new ones (i.e. if you attended one conference this year and found some great referrers, could you attend two next year, or three or four?)
10.	If you network, can you attend more events with the same or different providers?
11.	If you obtained referrers by direct marketing, can you do more of the same? For example, if you bought some data of ideal referral partners, can you either buy more data, or if you have used all the available data, can you target that same list again now?
12.	In all referral and client meetings, are you asking the magic referral question whenever anyone says what a great job you are doing/have done? **'Thank you. Is there anyone else you know who might benefit from my/our services?'**
13.	Do you do cross-promotions with other businesses who have a similar client base to your own? (For example, mentioning a seminar an accountant is running in one of your emails in return for the accountant mentioning you in one of his/her emails? This works well, as you are introduced by someone the prospect already trusts.)

The Google AdWords optimisation checklist

1.	Have you increased your AdWords budget? Google should provide a good return on investment, so if it is doing so, keep on in increasing your spend until you reach the maximum amount possible for your firm.
2.	Do you consistently run two split-test advertisements, rewriting the worst performer after around 500 impressions or more (sometimes even 100 if there is a clear winner)?
3.	Do you consistently move keywords out from large ad groups into their own smaller ad groups once they are working so that you can write more targeted advertisement content and improve your quality score and ad rank?
4.	Do you regularly run the 'search term' report to see the keywords that drove traffic to your website so that you can add good keywords and avoid bad ones by using 'negative' keywords?
5.	Do you use the Google AdWords keyword planner to come up with new ideas for keywords?
6.	Do you regularly look at Google Analytics to see what traffic is finding you organically (Login, then head to Acquisition/Search Console/Queries) and then add these keywords to your AdWords campaign to ensure that you are achieving maximum exposure? You might question why you would do this if you are showing organically already, but you will usually find that you are showing in positions too low in the results to gain any visits, and in any event, even if you are in position 1 organically that is actually position 5, as there are 4 AdWords advertisements before you now. Ideally you should be in position 1 in AdWords and also organically to get the largest volume and quality of visitors to your website.
7.	Do you consistently monitor your KPIs to notice any trends, good or bad? (I recently noticed that a client's average cost per click halved. The competition had stopped advertising. We were the only ones using AdWords in this niche so our costs dropped hugely!)
8.	Do you regularly improve landing pages to improve quality score and conversions?
9.	Does the content follow the PASTOR copywriting formula?
10.	Are the keywords included in the title tag, description tag, body content and image 'alt' and 'title' tags for that page?
11.	Is there enough content on the page to convince the visitor of expertise?
12.	Are there plenty of testimonials/reviews and case studies?
13.	Are there strong calls to action, with a variety of contact methods?
14.	Do you ensure that your keywords are in position one or two most of the time – anywhere else isn't really worth bothering with.

15.	Do you use call extensions, sitelink extensions and callout extensions as a bare minimum, to ensure that your advertisement is given the maximum number of lines?
16.	If you use these, do you regularly add new ones to improve your poorest performers?
17.	Do you use location targeting to weed out people from outside your service area?
18.	Do you use enhanced bids for the times of the day that your advertisements seem to convert best, or location enhancements for more local clients?
19.	Is your website mobile responsive (Chapter 10), to ensure you make the most of the rising number of mobile browsers?
20.	Do you use conversion tracking to ensure you know which of your keywords are generating the most enquiries?
21.	If you use conversion tracking, are you ensuring that your best performing keywords are always in position 1?

Chapter 15

Staying on Course for Continued Growth: Ensuring Your New Client Flowcast Stays Strong

I have given you everything that you need to grow your law firm. Well, almost. Practically, you have everything you need, but the truth is that that in itself is not enough. In addition to the practical formula, you also need to know some facts of life about running a law firm.

They are as crucial as the formula itself, because if you don't know about them, any one of them could derail your success at any time. I don't want that. I want you to be incredibly successful, so here is what you must know.

Step Away from Your Firm

Most solicitors are lucky if, when they come to sell their law firm they manage to achieve one year of turnover as their exit fee. Many achieve much less than this. Why is this, when, on the face of it, they have a profitable business?

In fact, this comes as no surprise to me, as most solicitors do not keep in touch with their clients once they have completed their business with them, so why should there be any loyalty to them?

That will of course be different for you now, as you will communicate with clients and referrers every month, but the others don't do this, which is why the 'good will' in their firms is practically non-existent.

There are only two reasons why law firms attract such low sale prices:

- they have no automated marketing methods in place to guarantee year-on-year growth; and
- they are totally reliant on their owners for their day-to-day running.

Everything I have covered so far in this book will resolve the first problem, and I'm now about to tell you what you need to do to remove the second one.

The easiest way to do this is to employ someone to run your firm for you. If you are currently a one-man band, this might be a few years ahead for you, but you need to know about it now so that you can plan for it in the long term.

If you are the main fee earner, your first aim must be to reduce, and then completely stop, fee earning as the starting point. If that idea terrifies you right now, this will change in time, I assure you. I have seen this happen so many times now that I know that once you start to have a business that is not totally reliant on you billing your clients, you will start to enjoy the different aspects of running your business.

Employing Staff

Step one for you is to employ someone else to fee earn as quickly as possible. Ideally you should employ someone in a junior position whom you can train to run matters in the same way that you do, as opposed to someone who wants to do everything in a completely random fashion because that keeps them engaged. If you want to build a firm that is easy to sell in the future, systematising and automating everything is a crucial part of the process.

When you employ staff, I strongly recommend that you establish a bonus system that rewards them when they do well, but one that also makes it very difficult for them to leave you. I first read about this bonus structure in John Warrilow's excellent book, *Built to Sell*. He recommends a bonus system that kicks in when certain financial targets are achieved (just like any bonus system) but – and this is the crucial part –, only one third of the total pot that a person has accrued is paid out to them in any given year. This genius system leads to a fee earner seeing a bigger and bigger bonus pot accruing each year, which gets harder and harder to leave behind if they do consider leaving your firm.

Crucially, it also takes away the need to offer your staff partnership. The last thing you want to do when growing your law firm is to give away your equity, as it makes it so much harder to be successful. Suddenly, every decision needs two heads, and someone who has no experience of running a law firm and, more importantly, has never taken a risk in their life but instead wandered into ownership of the firm that you created, slows down your progress.

It never ceases to amaze me how, even today, so many solicitors who are only good at one thing – being a solicitor – obtain partnership just by having been at a firm for a long time. They have done nothing over and above their basic day job, but because they have done this well enough, they put pressure on the owner to invite them into the partnership. When they do, all hell breaks loose. Suddenly they have a say in how the business is run. Now, you might think that their lack of experience would stop them from throwing in their two penn'orth, but you would be completely wrong. They will have an opinion about everything and will demand to be heard. They will ruin your business. Don't let them do it. Don't believe them when they say that they are going to go and set up on their own – 99% of them never will and those that do are more than likely going to fail.

You might be able to tell that this subject is close to my heart. It is. I believe in fairness. It isn't fair when someone who deserves nothing except their salary obtains partnership, throws their woefully inept weight about, and damages a good law firm. I have seen it happen too many times; don't let it happen to you.

Instead, use the bonus system I have suggested and let them build a growing pot that is only payable at one third of the bonus every year until the sale of your firm or their retirement. Linking it to the sale of your firm will also make it much more likely that they support you when the time does come for you to sell, because they will be financially motivated to do so. If you don't have such a scheme in place, however, when you try to sell your firm, your staff can quickly become demotivated. A pot of money awaiting them on sale reduces this risk.

Systems

Once you relinquish your fee-earning responsibilities, your next step is to systematise your management, marketing and financial processes, so that they are as streamlined as they can be.

At this point, once the profits have increased substantially, as they will do when everything is running smoothly, you will be able to afford to employ a managing director to run matters on a day-to-day basis, reporting directly to you and managing the staff on your behalf. You need to run through this process yourself first, so that you can manage your replacement and ensure that they maintain – or even improve – your standards. Ideally, when you come to recruit this person, I suggest you choose someone from outside the legal profession with proven experience at managing director level, preferably in a different professional services sector.

This will ensure that they bring new ideas to the table, instead of the same tired ideas that you will get if you employ someone who only has legal sector expertise.

> ### Making the change
>
> When I first suggested to John that he should stop fee earning he thought I was mad. He was the biggest fee earner in the practice by far, so the idea of losing those fees seemed extraordinary. However, within a couple of years he had stopped fee earning completely. It wasn't without its challenges, but the additional time and income it gave him to enjoy personal interests outside of it he found truly liberating.

Upsetting People

When you start taking action to grow your law firm some people will take offence. They might be your family, former clients, referral partners or so-called friends. Why will they do this? Change. People are terrified of change. They want you to stay exactly where you are right now. That way they know that everything is good. They can relax.

However, as soon as you start to do more marketing, they will notice that you are changing. The people most likely to take offence are those that you actually will not want as clients any longer. They will be the ones that pay the least for your services and moan the most. They will be referral partners who send you small amounts of work – nothing very profitable – yet they demand the world from you.

You need to understand this: if you never upset anyone with your marketing, I guarantee you will have a law firm that is pretty much stagnant in terms of growth.

You are going to have to suck in some air from time to time while people complain, but remember that this is a part of your growth as a person and as a law firm. You would be amazed at the number of people who stop doing any marketing the second anyone complains about it. However, this is great news for you. These are your competitors and if they keep doing what they have always done to promote their law firm (largely nothing), they will soon be out of business, leaving more instructions for you. The world no longer rewards law firms who take no positive action to market their services with a steady stream of instructions. Those days are long gone, so upset a few people.

Obviously, if the majority start to complain, you may well have overstepped the mark, but I have yet to see this happen.

Forewarned Is Forearmed

You have been forewarned, so if someone does complain, don't take immediate action, particularly when it comes to replying to the complainant. Sleep on it, read this chapter again, then sleep on it again. Then, in the cold light of two days later, analyse what you did, their response, and see how you feel now. In my experience, you will feel absolutely fine about it, particularly if, as I suggest above, the person who has complained is unlikely to be an ideal client or referrer for you now, so it is just time for them to move on.

Perfection Kills Momentum

When it comes to marketing your law firm, marketing needs momentum to thrive. If something is nearly there, if it is good enough, put it out there and get it working for you.

Marketing needs momentum – perfection kills momentum!

We are all so pressed for time, and while you may think that more time will open up tomorrow or next week to allow you to complete a marketing task, the truth of the matter is that any time that does open up will be swallowed up by another matter.

I often see this perfectionism putting the brakes on solicitors' marketing momentum in the following contexts.

Websites

Often a website is ready to be published and to generate new business for a firm of solicitors, only for it to be held back, awaiting final tweaking by one, two or three of the partners involved in the process. I have seen this final tweaking process take several months and in some cases over a year.

Every day that the website is not allowed to go live means missed opportunities to acquire new business. The website may be replacing an existing poor-quality website, or a new website for a firm without one. Either way, a good website live, published, and attracting visitors, even with some mistakes, is far better than a 'perfect' website gathering dust on your web design company's server.

Just publish the website!

Advertisements

When a new advertisement is drafted to replace an existing poor one, again, the final approval can take weeks or even months. Do not wait: publish the new advertisement and amend it when you have spotted where you can make improvements.

Direct Mail or Email Campaigns

A mailing campaign is a classic example of how something not being quite perfect can jeopardise an otherwise successful marketing campaign. Suppose you prepare a campaign and post or email your newsletter or direct mail to your database; 99% of the people that receive it have no problem with it, some even act on it and ask you to carry out some work for them – excellent.

However, one person out of the 1,000 that received it has moved, or worse still has since passed away. Their son or daughter calls you, and as you handled the probate, not surprisingly they are angry that you have sent a mail shot to their deceased parent. What do you do?

This is a real-life example from a law firm. What did they do? Well, this is all about perfection killing momentum: there will always be an error or two on a database, but sending the mailshot out was effective. So surely you apologise profusely, send a gift or make a donation as a mark of respect, amend the database so that the mistake does not happen again, and the problem is solved?

Not in this case: the senior partner decided never to send a mail shot to any client ever again. This one mistake (the database not being perfect) stopped everything.

Perfection kills momentum. You will make mistakes sometimes, but if you do nothing, always waiting for perfection, the major problem is likely to be that your practice goes out of business.

Advice

Be very careful who you take advice from, but when you pay a specialist for advice, take it.

I had to include some words on advice, because I have seen so many excellent plans stopped dead in their tracks because of it, or rather, lack of it. Without advice, you might stop yourself from achieving the growth that you desire. The self-sabotaging animal within you might derail your progress, and I don't want that to happen.

Please don't think this is just about my services. Yes, I've been through each of the scenarios below, but I have also seen this happen in countless other businesses outside of the legal profession, so my message is not just that you use my services and do everything that I tell you (although that would of course be an incredibly smart thing to do!), but that you should make the best use of advice.

Here are some of the reasons that I see a great plan derailed before it starts to pay dividends:

- The solicitor struggles to take advice because they are far more used to dishing it out.
- The solicitor's partners, who know less about growing a law firm than the solicitor tasked with growing it, stop the action being taken because they don't really understand it and decide to do nothing instead;

- The solicitor asks unqualified friends, family, website designers or junior 'fresh from college' marketing graduates for their opinion on what they are doing, and because their opinion is different from that of the 'scars earned' specialist who has spent years honing his or her skills, again they stop the activity.

The only 'judgement' on the advice should be the results that you achieve by carrying out the activity from start to finish. When you agree to test a marketing activity, agree an appropriate timescale, let it run, measure all of your results, and then decide whether to keep doing it. That is it.

Usually three months is enough for Google AdWords to show a return on investment, three advertisements are enough to show you if they make your telephone ring, six months of email marketing will show your referrals and recommendations going up, and 12 months of consistently adding unique, quality content to your website will show your visitor numbers and enquiries going up.

Be strong. If you take advice, see it through and then judge it solely on the results, not the opinions of others who have no grounds to provide an opinion in the first place.

Plotting Your Destination

Where exactly do you want your law firm to be? I have a very simple process for you to help you to reach your objectives. If you work alone, this is a very easy process. If you have many fee earners, it is the same process, it just has to be performed for each one of them.

First, let's start with the end in mind. Let's say for argument's sake that you want another £10,000 a month in fee income. How many additional instructions do you need to generate that fee income? Working on a £1,000 per transaction fee, that is 10 more instructions per month. Once you know that, life becomes so much easier: 10 more instructions per month, two per week or thereabouts. Now all you need to do is to work out where they are going to come from.

If you want them to happen instantly, you will need to use Google AdWords, as nothing gives you the speed that they do. You could use email marketing or regularly adding content to your website, but if you want that £10,000 a month within the next three months, then AdWords is the answer.

If you now know that you convert one in every two conveyancing enquiries into clients, because you are measuring these figures (Chapter 4), then you will need an additional 20 enquiries to land your 10 instructions.

Assuming the worst-case scenario with Google AdWords, you can expect two enquiries for every 100 clicks on your advertisements (often it is more than this), so you will need to generate 1,000 clicks per month. Tell your AdWords partner that that is your target, then just monitor their numbers as outlined in Chapter 11 and ensure that they deliver those clicks to you.

In a nutshell, that is it. It is and can be that simple. Yes, there may be some minor obstacles along the way, but that really is all you need to do to make the growth that you want to see happen.

As I said, if you want to do that for 10 fee earners, amplify the marketing by doing more of it to create the volume that you need for each fee earner in each department. Or make it work for one fee earner and then move onto the next, then the next…

The Five Stages of You, the Person and Law Firm Owner

STAGE 1: First, you have your parents. They make sure you do what you are supposed to do to live the life that at that point they want you to lead.

STAGE 2: Then you go to school. Now you have both your parents and your teachers to keep you on track, to make you do what you have got to do to be who they want you to be.

STAGE 3: Then you might go to university. Now the dynamic changes slightly. Your university lecturers want you to develop your own ideas and motivation – up to a point.

STAGE 4: Then you get a job, and both you and your employer decide what you need to do, with the final say coming down to the employer. Your parents may back down at this point, as you are living the life that they hoped you would, i.e. good profession, good job, steady pay, etc.

STAGE 5: Then one of two things is likely to have happened to get you to the point that you needed to pick up this book:

- you took over the firm that you have worked in for many years (or became an equity partner in it); or
- you decided that enough was enough; it was time to plough your own furrow, so you set up on your own.

Whichever of these two things applies to you, what is missing that you had in stages 1 to 4? Someone above you. A teacher or a boss. You may still have your parents – (as someone who has not long since lost one, I hope that you do), but by the time you reach Stage 5 you are plotting your own course.

Now who do you have to ensure that you do what you need to do to get the grades you want or to reach the billing target set? Who is going to hold you accountable? Since 2003, when I set up my business, I have realised that this point is vital if you are serious about growing your law firm quickly.

I assumed when I first set up my business that just because it was mine, because I had always had a very strong work ethic and made a lot of money for my employers, because everything that I did now was for my own benefit, it would all be supremely easy. It wasn't. Some days it still isn't.

I realise that this is exactly the same for all other business owners and law firm owners that I know. Left to our own devices we can fill the day but it is often at the expense of doing the things that we should be doing to get the results that we want to achieve.

One of my parting pieces of advice to you is to find someone to hold you completely accountable for achieving the goals that you have for your law firm. Agree with them what you are going to do, then check in with them at least on a monthly basis to see if you have done what you said you were going to do to achieve the targets that you have set for yourself.

You can do it on a quid pro quo basis with someone else you know in business, or you can pay someone to do it. Personally, I believe that unless you pay someone, and usually an amount that makes you feel a little uncomfortable, you will still slither out of doing all that you need to do. It is human nature. I follow my own advice, as always, so at the moment there are two businesses I pay to hold me accountable on different aspects of my own business. It works. If you find this book in your hands, the fact that I have finished it now when it has been in draft form for several years is proof that paying someone to hold you accountable works.

How You Start Your Day Matters – a Lot!

Let's go back in time and pretend that you have to hunt to feed yourself and your family every day. You live near a river, so fishing is your method of choice. What would be the first thing you did every day? It would be to grab your fishing rod and throw it in the water, wouldn't it?

Of course it would, because you would know that without the fish you wouldn't eat and if you went without food for a few days, your chances of living would decrease quite rapidly. The trouble now is that we have become far too comfortable. Food is easy to find; even if you don't have too much money, you can grab something to eat.

However, when it comes to running and growing your law firm, the same principles apply as they did with the fishing. You must fish first thing every day if you are serious about growing your law firm. Are you serious? Then prove it to me.

Tell me now, what is the first thing that you do every day when you come into your office? If you answered 'Well, first thing I check my emails, then when I get into the office I check the post, then I usually handle a few staff enquiries and before I know it it's 5 PM and time to go home', then I have some bad news for you.

You are never going to grow your law firm.

If you answered 'I get straight down to working on the marketing of my business', then fantastic. You will grow your law firm. You can't fail to. It is a certainty. Guaranteed. It really is that simple.

If you are going to let the rest of the world plan your day for you, responding to other people's demands on your time from emails, from post and from staff, then you are never going to grow your firm. You might get by or manage, but is that all you want? Really? If yes, then I suggest you quickly give this book to someone else who is serious about growing their law firm and go back to getting by, which is a phrase that makes me feel physically sick as I type it.

I told you at the beginning of this book that I was giving you the formula for success in growing a law firm, and I have done that. This final part is a huge part of it.

> **First thing, every day, you have to work on the growth of your law firm.**

I am not suggesting that this takes hours, usually 30 minutes a day is enough. Remember, the law firm growth formula teaches that you must outsource all of your marketing, so all your growth time will involve either running through your numbers, thinking about the next marketing artery to implement or improve, or coming up with some ideas for your next email newsletter, but these are all incredibly important and they do need some of your time.

Work on the marketing of your business first thing every day and you will succeed.

Your Success

I have given you a formula to follow here that works.

If you start having the meaningful conversation with your clients, put in place your marketing arteries from the New Client Flowcast and continually measure their performance and then optimise them, plus take yourself out of the process of 'doing' anything within your law firm, you can grow to whatever size your imagination will let you.

However, if you put this book down and say 'it had some interesting points, but I am going to keep on doing what I have always done', then the sad truth of the matter is that what you have always done doesn't work anymore. You have more competitors and it is much easier for clients to find them now, both online and offline. Your competition will be reading this book and taking action, because they are serious and committed about growing their practice.

Please don't fall into the trap that so many people do, as highlighted by the following conversation (an amalgamation of far too many conversations that I have had over the years).

CLIENT Nick, what new thing should I be doing now?

NICK Are you doing all of the things that I told you to be doing the last time we spoke? Are you sending an email newsletter to your ever-expanding client list, continually adding content to your website, using Google AdWords, tracking your referrals and rewarding your referrers?

CLIENT No, I stopped doing all of those things pretty much straight away after we stopped working together.

NICK Why?

CLIENT Well, I was quite busy, so I didn't see the need to continue marketing so I stopped it all. I saved myself some money by not spending on marketing (*said with pride*).

NICK Saved money? Why are you calling me now? Because you don't have enough work? You don't have enough work because you stopped the marketing

CLIENT No, it really isn't. The market is quieter and all sorts of other factors are involved.

NICK Sorry, that simply isn't true. All of my other clients who follow this plan and keep following it are as busy as they want to be. It is because you stopped doing what worked.

I wish I could say that this is an isolated conversation, but it isn't. I think because solicitors spend their entire life dishing out advice they sometimes find it hard to take advice themselves, always believing that they know better.

When it comes to marketing, unless you spend all day every day marketing your practice, you will never acquire the expertise that you need to grow your business to the levels that you desire, which is why you picked up this book to understand exactly what it is that you should be doing.

It is why I have shared my formula with you: to understand what needs to be done to acquire clients but then to outsource these activities, so that the work is done with or without you. All you need to do is to track the numbers each month and ensure that the marketing is providing you with an excellent return on investment. If it is, you keep doing it.

Don't fight yourself or press the self-sabotage button to stop doing marketing that is working. I cannot tell you the number of solicitors running successful, profitable Google AdWords campaigns providing a return on investment of five to one (i.e. £5,000 fee income on a £1,000 spend) who stop advertising because they become too busy or because their partners don't really understand how it works, so they simply pull the plug.

Let the people who do this be your competitors, because they won't be around for long. However, you will be if you follow the law firm growth formula.

Please do me a favour, though. When you do follow it, and it works, as it will do, please let me know. A client said he picked up some 'anger' in my voice when he told me recently that he had stopped doing all the marketing that was working for him. I explained that, yes, of course I was angry. In fact, more than angry, I was frustrated and upset.

The reason is because a lot of my job satisfaction comes from seeing my clients' successes. When I provide them with a formula, they follow it, and the law firm of their dreams develops before their eyes, I revel in it. So, when you take action and it works, as it will do, please do let me know. It will make my day. Thank you.

Resources

Finally, if you haven't already, please make sure you obtain all of the resources to make your life easier, including the following:

- the 'features to benefits' conversion form
- your three step service summary process
- the website design brief for obtaining the website you want at the price you should pay
- lead-tracking spreadsheet
- your KPI spreadsheet
- software website resources
- referral tracking spreadsheet
- marketing optimisation checklists

These are all available from www.samsonconsulting.co.uk /growth, so please go there and download them all now.

Acknowledgements

I would really like to thank every one of my clients. Without them, this book would simply not have been possible.

Without their willingness to try new marketing tactics and to consistently take action, I would not have been able to constantly test and improve my formula to reach the point that it was ready to publish in this book.

There are so many of you who I class as friends as well as clients and I sincerely thank you all. You are really good people. I wish you all the success that you crave and deserve in life.

Christelle, you have made my working life so much easier by being so well organised. Thank you.

My thanks also to my wonderful family that make everything I do so worthwhile.

I hope that this book gets you one step closer to understanding what it is that I actually do.

The Author

Nick is known as the fast growth marketing consultant to UK law firms, and regularly dispenses marketing advice to thousands of solicitors all over the country.

Having worked in the legal world for over 25 years, initially a solicitor and latterly as a consultant, Nick has a unique insight into what it takes to rapidly and profitably grow a law firm.

Renowned for increasing the turnover of more law firms than any other legal marketing consultant in the UK, Nick works closely with his private clients and 'Marketing4Solicitors' members to rapidly increase their turnover, profits and saleability.

You can find out more about Nick and contact him on:

Website – www.samsonconsulting.co.uk

LinkedIn – www.linkedin.com/in/nickjervis

Twitter – www.twitter.com/nickjervis

Printed in Great Britain
by Amazon